Under the Cloud

Under the Cloud

Dagmar E. Vasby
with
Charlene M. Luchterhand

Lur Publications
Danish Immigrant Archive

Dana College, Blair, Nebraska

Published by Lur Publications, Dana College, Blair, Nebraska, 68008.

First edition.

ISBN 0-930697-09-X

Second Printing

Logo designed by Elizabeth Solevad Nielsen
Designed by Thomas S. Nielsen, 2066 Colfax St., Blair, NE 68008
Printed by MicroSmart Printing & Graphics
                    1740 Washington St., Blair, NE 68008

Printed in the United States of America

Whenever the cloud lifted from above the tent, the Israelites set out; wherever the cloud settled, the Israelites encamped. At the Lord's command the Israelites set out, and at his command they encamped. As long as the cloud stayed over the tabernacle, they remained in camp. When the cloud remained over the tabernacle a long time, the Israelites obeyed the Lord's order and did not set out. Sometimes the cloud was over the tabernacle only a few days; at the Lord's command they would encamp, and then at his command they would set out. Sometimes the cloud stayed only from evening till morning, and when it lifted in the morning, they set out. Whether by day or by night, whenever the cloud lifted, they set out. Whether the cloud stayed over the tabernacle for two days or a month or a year, the Israelites would remain in camp and not set out; but when it lifted, they would set out. At the Lord's command they encamped, and at the Lord's command they set out. They obeyed the Lord's order in accordance with his command through Moses.

Numbers 9:17-23 (NIV)

Table of Contents

Illustrations   ix
Foreword   x
An Unusual Story   xi
Introduction   xiii

Chapter 1   Early Years   1
Chapter 2   Denmark   15
Chapter 3   Call to Mission   27
Chapter 4   China Mission   35
Chapter 5   Hardships Under the Japanese   43
Chapter 6   Soviet Occupation
                  and Chinese Civil War   59
Chapter 7   Leaving China:
                  He Led Us All the Way   65
Chapter 8   Around the World in 40 Years   79
Chapter 9   Homecoming   87
Chapter 10   Ganta Mission, Liberia   99
Chapter 11   New Directions   121
                  Epilogue - Special People   131
                  Acknowledgements   138
                  Glossary & References   139

Illustrations

Dagmar E. Vasby   xvi
Wedding picture of Dagmar's parents   3
Family picture   5
Marie and Dagmar's Confirmation Day   10
Dagmar as a student nurse in 1929   20
Family picture taken in 1930   21
Dedication Service for Dagmar   26
Teachers at the College of Chinese Studies   36
Chinese young people with Dagmar   42
Dagmar with co-workers at an orphanage   46
Chinese young people Dagmar worked with   49
The hospital in Antung   52
Dr. Li   53
Nurses and student nurses caring for babies   62
Dr. Li and Dagmar at the hospital   64
Olsen family walked out of China with Dagmar   66
Danish Christian Lutheran Church Document   72
Letter in Chinese from Ai Zhen   82
Niels Christian Petersen, 1940   88
Map of Ganta Mission   98
Bridge from Monrovia to Ganta Mission   102
Dagmar with Dr. Harley's assistants   104
Mildred Black and patients at Ganta Mission   106
Leper Colony in 1952   106
Dagmar treating a patient at Ganta Mission   108
Dagmar traveling to work at Ganta Mission   108
Ganta Mission School students in new outfits   112
Dagmar in Africa in 1950   114
Two men who burned their fetishes   116
Sei Punagbea   119
Dagmar with Dr. Sekenene and Dr. Ross   124
Dagmar with two nurses at Bomi Hills   124
Laura and Niels Christian Petersen anniversary   128
Dagmar and Joe Vasby's wedding picture   130
Vasby family, 1955   136
Joe and Dagmar Vasby with their children, 1980   136
Grandchildren and great-grandchildren, 1993   137

Foreward

Jesus invited men and women to follow him. His intention was to give to each one the happiest, holiest, hardest and most hopeful possible life. The Bible says, "Life in all its abundance." When we find women and men who have accepted that invitation and have done so willingly and with fierce passion, their lives inspire, confront, encourage, convict and haunt us. This book is about such a life.

Dagmar Vasby began her journey in small towns in the cold part of north-central America. She moved to Denmark at age 15 with her Lutheran minister father and family. Her father had responded to the call from Denmark for pastors. It was in the very late 1930's as Hitler was coming into power. She became a nurse and missionary. Dagmar was in China when the Japanese invaded and was still there when the Chinese Communists took control. She was among the very last Danish missionaries out of Manchuria. What happened there reads like the book of Acts.

Later God led her to Liberia where she was the first nurse in a Methodist mission hospital. I have seen, first hand, the work done at that hospital and the hope engendered in the hopeless.

Then, a strange and wonderful turn of events led her into a whole new adventure in the United States.

My wife and I stayed in the home of Dagmar several years ago. At nearly four in the morning I had to make a night journey, and it led me through the kitchen. She was there at a modest table with a large map, her Bible, some literature, and a list of missionaries. She was petitioning God on behalf of colleagues, friends, and people she did not know, who were responding to the call of God to all parts of the world to bring the love of God and the Good News of the gospel. It moved me to see her there, at that very early hour, living out her passion to live with, to love, and to serve Jesus Christ.

Dagmar has given to each of us a very remarkable gift that will leave its indelible mark - the story of her life.

Howard Hovde
Director Emeritus, Laity Lodge

An Unusual Story

A few times before I've been asked to read manuscripts by individuals or family members who believe their story merits publication. I have generally concluded that such stories would have limited interest to readers beyond immediate family members and friends. *Under the Cloud* will have wider appeal. I was originally drawn to the story because it features the early life of the daughter of a Danish minister and his wife. The minister, Rev. Christian Petersen, came to America to pursue his undergraduate education and theological training in Blair, Nebraska, at Dana College and Trinity Seminary, the college I now serve as President.

This is the story of a remarkable woman, Dagmar Petersen Vasby. The book opens with a brief sketch about her grandparents and parents and continues with Dagmar's birth in America's heartland in 1907. When her parents returned to their homeland, Denmark, Dagmar was 15. Having grown up with the Danish language and customs, she had little difficulty adjusting to her new home among family members in Denmark. Following nurses training and employment as a surgical nurse, Dagmar accepted a call from the Danish Lutheran Mission Board to serve as a nurse in their mission field in China (Manchuria). This meant difficult and potentially dangerous travel by the Trans-Siberian railway through Russia. Throughout her stay in a country occupied first by the Japanese and then the Russians, she survived disease, tyranny, and other hardships and dangers experienced by few of her countrymen. After her return to Denmark following another visit to the land of her birth, Dagmar accepted another call. This time, 1949, her journey was to Africa (Liberia) where she would face new challenges as a nurse and administrator in an unfamiliar culture. As was her experience in China, Dagmar grew to love the people she served. Additional education and responsibilities in Denmark and Africa filled the ensuing years for this remarkable woman. The narrative ends in August of 1954 with Dagmar's marriage to Joe Vasby at the cathedral in Aarhus, Denmark. Joe was a widower with five children from Cambridge, Wisconsin, the community where she stayed many times on her prolonged visits to America. In Cambridge her Christian witness and service has continued for nearly a half century.

Dagmar's story is skillfully told with the assistance of her co-author, Charlene Luchterhand. Together, they capture the reader's interest, leaving one eager to learn the outcome of each new adventure. *Under the Cloud* is important for its insider story of how World War II touched the lives of the poor, the ill, and the common in remote as well as heavily populated places. It took courage and faith for a young woman from Europe and America to travel to and in Asia and Africa when travel on those continents was often uncomfortable, unsafe, and unreliable.

Important to her story, Dagmar's is a life informed and shaped by her Christian faith. In a time when many find the faith narrative out of fashion or politically incorrect, *Under the Cloud* is refreshing. To those who question whether God is active in shaping people and events, Dagmar's story is compelling testimony. Hers is a heart-warming account of a dedicated Christian who loves all of God's people, meets difficult challenges, and endures uncertainty, loss and separation confident that God will sustain, comfort, and provide.

I believe readers will share my pleasure in this work. Like the Israelites, Dagmar followed the cloud, obeying the Lord's call to love, respect, and serve strangers. In an era when few women ventured far from family and friends, Dagmar lived on four continents. Hers is a story worth reading.

Myrvin F. Christopherson, Ph.D.
President, Dana College

Introduction

She sat down across the table from my husband and me at a potluck dinner prior to a Lenten Service. I had met Dagmar Vasby briefly before and always received a welcoming smile and squeeze of the hand when I would sit near her during Sunday morning church services. This time, though, we had more time to talk. Leaving a table filled with her friends, she joined us as we sat alone, the newcomers to the church. "I want to get to know you better," the silver-haired nonagenarian said. Surprisingly, the direction our conversation took would send Dagmar and me on an ambitious joint venture for the next year.

As my husband talked about his career as a computer programmer, Dagmar expressed frustration with her own computer skills. "I've been asked by so many people to write about my life, " she said, "but I guess it's not meant to be. I'm having too many problems working with my computer. I guess at my age, I shouldn't expect to write anymore." Recently unemployed after funding for my position in medical research was cut, I found myself saying, "I have some time right now. Could I help you?" "Char has had a book published, you know," my husband added. Dagmar had heard enough. That very night following the Lenten service she asked if we would stop at her home. Once there she filled my arms with her diaries and written drafts of some of her life experiences. Sampling them, I was hooked immediately. I quickly learned that this unassuming woman had lived a rather extraordinary life as a medical missionary during a critical time in the world's history.

She called two countries, Denmark and the United States, "home" and had lived also in China and Liberia. She had sailed across the Atlantic seven times and had flown more times than that. Much of this intercontinental travel took place well before the jet age when such travel became commonplace for business people and vacationers.

I was awestruck as Dagmar described what she saw as she traveled by train through Siberia during the time of Stalin's great purge. I was amazed at the great danger she had faced in her life. Unjust warrants were issued for her arrest in China, and twice a gun was held to her chest. Five months elapsed as she tried to flee China following World War II. In Liberia, she found herself alone in the midst of the jungle one night when the car in which she was a passenger broke down. I learned world history that I had not known before. I was touched by Dagmar's compassion for others and inspired by her faith. I found my own faith renewed as she provided evidence of God's love and direction in her life and the lives of others.

Dagmar's life unfolded as we met weekly in her homey kitchen. Fortified with hot tea in winter and cold drinks in summer, I listened and questioned, took notes and tape-recorded. Oftentimes, Dagmar wrote out her experiences longhand and then read her drafts to me. Encouraged by my interest and enthusiasm, Dagmar continued to reminisce. We pored over yellowed photo albums, and looked up scripture passages. We edited and revised and continued to add content. Gradually highlights from the first half of her life emerged in written form.

Dagmar's years as a medical missionary were full and eventful. She had the privilege of getting to know many interesting people of different nationalities and cultures. Yet, it is not so much Dagmar's story that we want to tell, as it is the love story as old as life itself — the love of God for the people He created. This is a story of belief in the Lord and the lifelong influence of loving, Christian parents. It is a story about stepping out in faith, not feeling fully prepared for the tasks ahead, but trusting in the Lord to provide guidance along the way. It is a description of the incredible life journey that can happen through faith and trust in God. I hope that Dagmar's story will inspire you and provide reassurance for you through difficult times. I hope that your faith will be strengthened by her example and God's demonstration of His great love. Blessings!

Charlene Luchterhand

Dagmar E. Vasby

1

The early years

Train a child in the way he should go, and when he is old he will not turn from it. Proverbs 22:06 (NIV).

Laura and Christian

My narrative begins in Denmark in the 1800s, years before my birth. In that small, beautiful country lived two individuals who would become the most influential people in my life.

Laura Nielsen was born in Denmark on September 7, 1876. Her father was a very good and prominent tailor who sewed for the rich and famous of the Jutland area. Laura's mother had been born into an aristocratic family. Although her grandmother had been disinherited for marrying below her class, Laura's mother acted lady-like to her dying day. She was gracious, refined, always neatly dressed, and carefully controlled in any display of emotions.

Laura was the second born of four children, three girls and one boy. She was an intelligent child and learned to read at an early age. She had a critical health problem however - a serious case of tuberculosis (TB). Doctors told the family numerous times that Laura would die "when the leaves fall." With characteristic optimism, Laura would say, "What leaves?" The illness kept Laura out of school so much that she had a tutor in her home. Often her mother would find her underneath her bed where she would be hiding with a book. Laura seemed to have a zest for life that was quite unusual, and despite the illness, her mother managed to have her take dancing lessons and to have her ears pierced. These activities were unusual for a member of a Christian family and hinted at the family's cultured background.

When Laura was a teenager, a spiritual revival occurred in Denmark. Thousands of young people gathered around the country for religious meetings, which often focused on foreign missions. Laura learned that such meetings were being held in the Mission House near her home. She had been confirmed in the church and now had a desire to learn more about God. One day, as she was walking home alone from one of the youth meetings, she left the road, knelt down behind the roadside ditch and dedicated her life to Christ. At the time her parents did not understand this commitment.

For several years, fellowship conferences were held for Danish youth; these were very well-attended. In 1895, when Laura was 18, the gathering was convened on June 5 - 7, in the area surrounding Holstebro on Denmark's west coast. An estimated 7000 young people attended the conference. None of the churches or buildings was large enough to hold all the participants so the meetings were conducted outdoors in a field that was offered by a local resident. The area was decorated with flagpoles, and flowers graced the dais and pulpits. Many prominent ministers spoke, and the crowd was wildly enthusiastic. On the third day of the conference a trip to the ocean was planned. The weather was beautiful and 650 young people participated in this event. On the first leg of the trip, the participants traveled by train, staying overnight with friends in the area. The next day area farmers supplied over 100 wagons to take the young people the rest of the way to the ocean. Laura was on one of those wagons.

Before Laura had started out on this trip, she had had a dream in which she had seen a handsome young man walking toward her across a field. While she was sitting in the wagon waiting for others to climb on board, she looked up and there was the image again, only this time it was no dream! The drive to the ocean took a couple of hours. The young people were all filled with enthusiasm about the wonderful fellowship they had enjoyed during the past two days. They talked and sang all the way to the ocean. But the trip was even more special for Laura and Christian, the young man who had jumped into the wagon, and before the excursion was over, they had promised each other that they would keep in touch. It had been love at first sight!

Who was the young man who so totally captured Laura's heart? Christian Petersen was born on January 30, 1876, to parents who operated a small farm. His father was also a carpenter and for a time, a guard at the royal palace in Fredensborg. Christian was the third oldest of six children, three girls and three boys. He was a quiet, industrious child. When he was only seven years old, he worked away from home on neighboring farms. This was commonplace for the children of small farmers, who could not afford to keep them at home. Christian decided at a very young age to become a minister, and at the age of 10 or so, he could be found preaching to the cows or the neighbor children. At that time it was difficult to obtain higher education in Denmark. Christian's friends encouraged him to go to the U.S., and although he could not speak English, he was accepted into Dana College in Blair, Nebraska, a college founded as an institution of higher learning for young Danes.

Shortly before Christian left for the U.S., he and Laura became engaged. Christian wrote to Laura that if their love were true, it could wait. He threw himself into his studies, first having to learn the English language, and to sup-

2

Wedding picture of Dagmar's parents,
Niels Christian and Laura Petersen. Married July 12, 1904

port himself through school, he took any job he could get. He helped on farms, worked in a nursery, and taught Danish in various congregations. Laura also made good use of her time while waiting for Christian. She completed an apprenticeship and began to earn her living by sewing. She had an advantage since her father had already established such a good reputation as a tailor in the community, and her work brought her into a multitude of homes where she made many new friends. In the home of a minister she not only gained friends for life, but also received guidance in her life as a Christian and in preparation for her future role as a pastor's wife. Laura's mother did all she could to turn her daughter's mind away from the young man who had left for a foreign country, and she arranged introductions to some very eligible young men. However she soon realized that her beloved daughter was just as strong-minded as she was. Laura firmly believed that God's plan for her life was to wait for Christian and marry him when he returned.

Letters between the two were slow coming and going between the continents, but when they did arrive they were filled with love and dedication. Seven long years passed with not even one visit between the couple. However the long wait was finally over. Christian had finished his studies at the Theological Seminary at Dana College and had graduated with honors. It was a very exciting day for them when they finally embraced after so many years of waiting. The wonderful reunion was marred, however, by the unhappiness of Laura's parents. Christian needed to return to Dana College for his ordination, and Laura's parents refused to assist her in joining him; so she sold her belongings, and with her meager savings they set off for their new life across the ocean. Christian left Laura in the care of dear friends in Boston as he went on ahead to prepare a place for her to live until they could be married. She continued to support herself through her sewing.

Christian was ordained on June 5, 1904, and the long-awaited wedding occurred one month later on July 12. Friends in Staplehurst, Nebraska, helped them plan the special event. Christian had received several calls from congregations ranging from Nebraska to Maine but accepted a call from a small congregation in Potter, Nebraska, believing that the warm, dry prairie air would be best for Laura, who still suffered from bouts of coughing and hemorrhaging from the TB she had had as a child. Praying and trusting the Lord, they set up their first household. As they sat down to their first meal, Christian said with a sigh, "To think I am putting my feet under my own table!" Many joys and hardships awaited them, but as long as they had each other, they were ready to face everything that came their way with great confidence.

A New Experience for Laura

Laura's new lifestyle was quite lonely at times. The Danish community was very widespread, and for a pastor that meant long hours on the road since his means of transportation was the horse and buggy. Christian's salary was paid in part by material goods. Topsy, a beautiful black horse with a white star on her forehead, became part of his salary and she proved to be a very valuable asset for many years to come. While Topsy helped Christian travel to his parishioners, Laura kept busy sewing and learning the new language.

A home on the American prairie was very different from her home in the beautiful and luxurious Danish Jutland area where Laura had lived most of her life. It was easy to become lost on the prairie. One day when Christian was out visiting parishioners, a severe snowstorm came up. He completely lost his bearings and wandered about alone and confused until suddenly he saw a

4

Family picture: Niels Christian, Marie, Dagmar and Laura

light in the distance and decided to follow it, not knowing that the light shone from his own home and that inside sat his beloved Laura anxiously waiting and praying for his safe return. Another day when Laura was alone, she was startled by a strange roaring noise, and she rushed outside to find a herd of wild horses stampeding around the house. These adventures certainly would not have happened in well-populated Denmark!

The Family Grows, and I arrive

While Laura and Christian eagerly awaited the birth of their first child, Laura sewed and embroidered 24 white dresses for the little one to wear. That first little baby, Marie, born on September 26, 1905, was a frail little girl who was cared for tenderly by her parents. In the meantime Laura gained a companion; a young girl who was being tutored for confirmation stayed at the parsonage and helped out so she did not have to travel back and forth to her home.

Shortly after Marie's birth the small family moved temporarily to Moorhead, Iowa, where I was born, and then to Cordova, Nebraska, so they would be closer to the seminary. I came along on February 12, 1907, less than 17 months after Marie was born. While Marie was never robust, I was healthy and a little tease, or so I later was told by my baby-sitter. My parents, however, never made me feel that I had been a rascal. My dad did tell me later, as I accompanied him on errands, that I was the one who always had to do the talking. He also told me that if Marie fell, she would just lie there until I came along to pick her up. I tell these anecdotes to describe the close bond that formed between Marie and me. We became a team. As the oldest of what would become a family of nine children, we always worked together and roomed together. We even wore identical clothes, except that she wore blue to match her eyes and I wore pinks and reds. My clothes, however, were always dirty before hers and never seemed to last as long.

The family's third child and first son, Emil, was born in Cordova. The parsonage was close to the church and located in the center of the town; therefore, many things were now more convenient for them. Laura was always busy sewing, but she also entertained and took part in church life. Christian took great pride in his firstborn son. Family stories tell of little Emil folding his hands during prayer time when he was only eight months old. Tragedy struck soon afterwards when Emil became sick and died. The congregation grieved along with the family.

During the following year, 1910, a third daughter, Helga was born, and the family thanked God for this healthy child. In 1911, the family of five moved to Trufant, Michigan. The trip was exciting to Marie and me because Dad was always pointing out various wonders of nature. It was fun; we never knew what he would show us next. One night he woke us from a sound sleep. "You must see the Mississippi River," he said.

Trufant, Michigan

Trufant was a small community of Danish immigrants. The town was named after Emory Trufant, who was the first person to buy land there. When we arrived in 1911, Trufant was a thriving community. It had a post office, sawmill, furniture store, drugstore, grocery store and a railroad which ran through town carrying lumber to the sawmills. The cutting of white pine in northern Michigan was big business. As the hardwood trees were cleared away, the stumps were pulled up and placed on their sides with the roots in the air, the roots were connected to each other to make fences for the fields. The immigrants were good farmers and hard workers. It was said that even into the forties and fifties there had never been a crime committed in the vicinity.

The Danish Lutheran Church was built in 1893 as a one-room building heated by a pot-bellied stove. The pews were made by hand and adorned with hand-carved decorations; the organ, a wind instrument requiring air to produce sound, was pumped by the custodian. The previous pastor, who was a good carpenter, had helped to build the church. An altar was built in 1902, and a beautiful altar picture of Peter sinking in the waves, painted by a man named Andersen, made a big impression on my young life. In 1919 the church was remodeled and two wings were added.

In Trufant, Christian and Laura became seasoned leaders of the people,

6

whom they seemed to love. It was here also that I first began to realize that Christian and Laura were two very special people and that I was quite privileged to have them for my parents. I hope my story will help demonstrate how their example had a lifetime influence on their children.

My parents referred to their hobbies as the three b's - børn, blomster og bøger - Danish words for children, flowers and books. There were always flowers in our gardens and indoors in pots and vases. Like the flowers, our family also continued to grow. Two boys, Bernhard and Richard, and three more girls, Esther, Grace, and Ruth, joined the fold. The doctor who delivered Esther wanted to adopt her, but Mother always said that they did not have one child too many, even if her doctor thought so! Esther became the family's role model. Among all the chattering girls, she was the listener. I do not recall her ever needing to be reprimanded.

Richard was a curly-headed blond little fellow who was full of mischief. He was a handful for Marie and me to watch over as we played because he was always inspecting something or walking away from the rest of us if something caught his attention. He was hard to keep clean. One day he got into the shoe shine box and ended up with black shoe polish all over his hair and clothes before we found him. Another time he got into the chicken yard with a couple of his younger sisters; they ran around trying to catch the rooster, chasing him until the poor bird died. On another occasion when I was walking home from the store with one of my parents, we found Richard and the three younger girls sitting on the ridge of the roof. They had climbed out of a bedroom window, onto a porch roof and then up to the next level. Somehow Mother and Dad always saw the humor in such situations and were able to warn us about safety issues without anger or spanking.

The parsonage was large. There was a bathroom containing a sink and bathtub, but no hot running water. We used a pump in the small kitchen to draw water from a cistern which stored rainwater, and we then carried the water into the bathroom. Like most everyone else at the time, we had an outhouse in back. A large room upstairs served as a wonderful playroom for us and the neighbor children, who were always welcome. Here we put on plays and invited others to watch. One advantage of being in a large family was that we always had playmates.

We did not own a telephone, and of course there was no television at that time. But plenty of books lined the shelves of the study from floor to ceiling. There was no electricity, but there were gas-operated ceiling lights. In the evening we gathered around the large table to do our homework, and after that we played games. We started early each year to make decorations for the Christmas tree. We were all taught to make colorful baskets that were traditional Danish hearts made of two different colors of glazed paper. I was not very handy at this type of craft compared to Marie. Watching her made me want to give up and do other things while she plugged away at the decorations. She certainly inherited Mother's talent with needles, crochet hooks, and other crafts. By the age of 12, she could sew her own clothes. I helped with the

7

heavier physical work and felt more comfortable washing dishes and doing housework. For outdoor activities, we had swings and a trapeze, all hand-made by Dad. We also played ball and a game called sticks so there was never time to get bored.

I do not remember when the organ came into our home; it seems that it was always there. When Marie was eight years old, a woman came to the parsonage to give her lessons, but I was expected to wait another year before starting. I wanted so much to take lessons with Marie that I quietly left the room to get my report card, and showing her my grades, I asked the woman if she agreed that I could learn also. She did agree, and my parents gave in. I loved to play the organ. Dad and Mother were both very good singers, and singing was always a part of our lives. They taught us many beautiful songs and hymns.

My father's salary was very meager. In 1915, it was only eight hundred dollars a year, supplemented by gifts of food from the congregation. When the farmers butchered, they would bring us meat, which had to be preserved by canning because there was no refrigeration. We were poor but we did not know it, since our parents were thrifty and resourceful. My mother, who was often "under the weather," either pregnant or feeling the long-term effects of TB or both, never gave up. We were all scrubbed and clean and among the best-dressed in school. We took this for granted until Dad pointed out how differ-ent life would have been without Mother's talents. Mother often sewed into the wee hours of the morning fashioning clothing for us from donated hand-me-downs.

Dad was a dedicated minister who often had to be away from home, leav-ing mother alone with us children. Yet he watched over her and did all he could to help. He would serve her breakfast in bed and then arouse the army of children. When Dad came home from his ministerial duties, he would milk the cow, feed the horse and chickens, and keep the large yard neat. He always maintained a sizeable vegetable garden, and he helped Mother with the laun-dry. Fortunately Dad was young and strong!

Dad saw to it that we all helped Mother. All the children, no matter how young, were assigned tasks to complete, and as we got older, Marie, Helga, and I would sometimes get up in the middle of the night to set the table or do some cleaning when Mother was worn out. We would then sneak back to bed so no one knew we had been up. The children also contributed to the family income by helping to harvest potatoes in the fall. Michigan was an important potato-growing state; school was recessed for two weeks every fall so that chil-dren could pick up and crate the potatoes that had been dug earlier with the use of horse-drawn equipment. It was a back-breaking job and often done when it was quite cold outside, but we earned money for our winter outfits in this way.

As we children reflect on those days, we all agree that it was a very well-organized household. Mother and Dad were a team, but opposite from each other in some respects. Dad smiled mostly with his eyes, while at times Mother

8

would laugh until tears ran down her cheeks. Dad showed quiet concern about things, but Mother seemed carefree. She always quoted scripture, answering any challenge that seemed insurmountable with, "Hitherto the Lord has helped us and He will help us again." Love between our parents was very evident, and their love for us children was sacrificial and real. We always knew that our parents appreciated us and our contributions to the family. I remember one occasion when Dad came quietly into the kitchen and took a dish towel out of my hands and encouraged me to join a ball game outside. We did what our parents told us to do without grumbling because of the loving atmosphere.

On Saturday mornings Dad taught Danish school to the people who were eager to preserve their native language. They learned Danish history and to read and write in Danish. Despite being poor we always had enough money to help others if they needed food or clothing. Some girls who lived on the outskirts of the community would stay overnight after attending Danish school. One girl was very poor. Mother sewed her confirmation dress, and Dad bought her other clothes. She looked as good as any of the others. It was this type of ministry that endeared them to their congregation.

Dad practiced what he preached. One day we older girls felt very indignant that a neighbor had snubbed our father, and we mentioned it to Dad. He seemed very thoughtful when this subject was brought to his attention. He must have conferred with Mother because a short while later he asked us to invite that neighbor and his wife for afternoon coffee. On another occasion when I was in second grade and Marie in third, the teacher reprimanded me when some other children were scuffling as we were lined up to leave for the day. I didn't say anything, but when Marie reached the door where the teacher was standing, she said, "Dagmar did not push anybody. It was someone else." Later that day feeling very proud that Marie had proved my innocence, I told Dad what had happened. Dad answered, "What did you do? Did you sass back to your teacher? Now you can both go down the street to apologize." Oh! It was awful, but we did it. Many years later, I visited Trufant as an adult. The teacher was still living and remembered the incident that had endeared us to her.

A new barn belonged to the parsonage; this accommodated our cow, Filey, and our horse, Topsy, who had traveled on the train with us from Nebraska. Topsy had a personality all her own. She knew she was a family pet and was ready to take us wherever we needed to go in winter or summer, but she had different ideas about working for others. When she put on too much weight in summer, Dad would loan her out to local farmers to do some work. Invariably Topsy would find her way home at night, lift the latch to the barnyard and would be standing there in the morning waiting for us. After this happened a few times, she was allowed to stay at home. When Dad spoke to her, she seemed to understand what he said. One cold winter night we were driving home from a service in one of the outlying areas where a few Danish families lived. I was upset because I had forgotten my precious fur muff. As we turned around to retrieve the lost item, Topsy balked and slowly dragged her feet. Dad said

Marie and Dagmar's Confirmation Day, May 16, 1920

to her, "Now, Topsy, if you will be good and get going, I will give you an extra bag of oats." Believe it or not, she took off!

In a large family, sickness could hardly be avoided. We were never encouraged to complain or be sissies, but if we were really ill, we were cared for by both of our parents. Since Mother still felt the effects of her childhood TB, she believed in prevention. For us this meant cod liver oil on a regular basis and plenty of fresh air. The windows were always open at night while we slept, even on cold winter nights. Sometimes we woke to find snow on our windowsills! At the age of eight I became very ill with a kidney infection. I remember waking from a coma with my mother sitting at my side. She asked how I felt about dying. I was rather surprised because the thought of dying had never entered my mind. After six weeks I was able to sit up in a chair. My teacher came to visit me and caught me sneaking out of bed to see what was going on outside. I was old enough to wonder if she thought that I was too well to stay home from school. I returned to school but felt weak for months. I was a little embarrassed when the teacher would ask if I felt all right.

I have a dear memory from a church service during this time. We were all taught and expected to sit still and listen in church even at a very young age. Mother had a baby on her lap and a little one on her left side. I felt tired and leaned my head on her arm. I fell asleep and woke thinking how good my mother was to allow a big girl like me to lean on her and sleep in church. This sense of love and security shaped our young lives for the days to come.

We learned when very young to take everything to God in prayer, both individually and as a family. Each morning began with a time of devotions around the big dining room table. On Saturday nights after bath time we would kneel at Mother's knees to say our prayers. Every Sunday morning we would find a clean set of clothes ready for us to wear to church laid out on a chair. Dad always gave us pennies for the offering plate before we headed off to Sunday School. A tithing box was kept in his study to collect money for missions.

Confirmation instruction was started at the age of thirteen. Classes were held in the study in the parsonage for a period of two years. In May, 1920, Marie and I were confirmed together even though I had received only one year of instruction. We asked to be confirmed together because we had shared so many things. We often prayed together about things we alone knew. Dad granted our request to be confirmed together after he consulted with other pastors. One reason we got our wish was that after nine years in Trufant, Dad had accepted a call from a congregation in McNabb, Illinois, and we would be leaving Trufant in November. Confirmation was a meaningful day of commitment for us. To the extent that I could understand, I wanted to follow Jesus.

In October, before we moved to Illinois, the last of our siblings, Naomi, was born. Marie and I took a special interest in her because we had found Mother crying at the beginning of her pregnancy. When we asked why she was crying, she explained that she was pregnant again and that Marie and I had been baby sitters so much, she did not want us to do that any more. We tried to comfort her with the assurance that we did not mind that role and would gladly help her. I believe we were totally honest and always loved our younger sisters and brothers. As it turned out Naomi brought much love into our family, and it was she who continued to care for our parents in their old age.

11

A Boyfriend

McNabb, Illinois, was a wealthy community located in an area of rich farm land. Several families owned cars! Most area residents were generous, and Dad's salary increased from $800 a year in Trufant to $1000, which seemed to make a difference in our lives. It was a good climate in which to be preacher's kids, "P.K.s" as we were called. The church was quite new, having been re-built recently after the previous one was destroyed by fire. The one problem we had was space; we went from living in a large parsonage to a very small one. We did not mind being a little crowded; we still made room for guests at times and enjoyed having friends at our house.

Leaving Michigan was not an easy move for any of us, but the people of McNabb were friendly and caring. It did not take long for us to adjust to our new circumstances. I was about to start my sophomore year and Marie her junior year of high school. Only two years of high school were held in McNabb, then the junior and senior students went to Swaney high school about two miles away. As always, Marie and I wanted to be together, but this could only be accomplished if I moved in with a family in the Swaney district, since I was not yet a junior. I moved in with a farm couple who did not have any children, and I did chores for them to pay for my room and board. This also helped ease the crowded living conditions at home. For this same reason, and also to earn money for clothing, Marie and I took jobs in homes during summer vacations.

When I was fourteen years old, I fell head-over-heels in love! George was five years older than I and he was already out of high school, helping his Dad on their farm. His family, the Andersen's, had nine children just like we did, and also like us, had two boys and seven girls. The Andersens were older; the youngest of them was the same age as Marie, the oldest in our family. Mr. and Mrs. Andersen were pleased that we were friends with their family and were extremely good to us. We spent many wonderful hours with the family play-ing all kinds of games, riding horses, and exploring the woods. Mrs. Andersen was a large woman with a very big heart. When we went to her home, she would throw her arms wide open and give us big hugs. The older Andersen girls were counselors for our church youth group, and when we went on out-ings or to camp, they would go along. A sizable group of young people be-longed to the church, and we were fortunate to have a good youth program. Music was another activity we shared with the Andersens. All of the Andersens were great singers. Marie and I sang in the church choir and continued to play the organ.

I was only fourteen when I started dating George, but I was very mature. He had a new model T ford and would often offer me a ride after Sunday evening services in the summer to the home where I would be working the following week. My parents allowed this until the woman of the house told my father that I was staying out too late. The next Sunday night Dad hitched Topsy to the wagon and stood ready to drive me back. I told him that George was going to take me back. "Not tonight," he said quietly, "I hear you cannot get in on time." No more was said and no more was necessary. I got the message and so did George. It did not stop our love for each other however; love always finds a way.

A life-changing decision

One spring day in 1922 Marie and I were out on the school lawn with our friends at recess when we saw Dad drive up in the horse and buggy. He had come to talk with us about a surprising subject. My parents had received an invitation to return to Denmark! After World War I there was a campaign underway in the United States to speak only the English language. This was no problem for my parents because they had become bilingual. Several pastors from other Danish churches, though, decided it was time for them to turn over their congregations to the younger generation and return to their homeland. They encouraged Dad to return with them. My mother had always followed Dad wherever he went without considering the cost to herself. She wanted him to make the choice so she was very careful about voicing her opinion, yet to return to Denmark would be a dream come true for her. My parents had not been back to Denmark since they left prior to their marriage. My mother's parents were about to celebrate their 50th wedding anniversary so it would be a special time for them to return. Dad determined that the decision would be up to Marie and me. If we did not want to go, my parents would drop the matter entirely. Marie and I were taken completely by surprise and had a limited time to make this big decision!

2

Denmark

Unless the Lord builds the house, its builders labor in vain. Psalm 127:1 (NIV).

I will never say good-bye again!

The decision was made - we would all move to Denmark! We had a very eventful summer. Marie and I took jobs in the same home in Evanston, Illinois; she was the cook, and I, the baby-sitter. We were very lonely that summer, but it was a good way for us to earn some money for travel clothes. During this time, Marie and I continued to learn about the value of praying together and for each other in all circumstances. One day when I was taking the little girl for a stroll, Marie felt very anxious for me. When I returned home, she asked where I had been and told me about her inexplicable concern. Her worry was well-founded, although she could not possibly have known that. As I was walking around the block, I became aware that I was being followed. A man would precede me down the road in his car and then stop until I caught up with him. This went on for some time, and I became very suspicious of his motives. When he took off again, I pushed the stroller faster and hurried home through an alley and some back roads.

When Marie and I returned to our home, I had to marvel at the way Dad and Mother organized for the move to Denmark. There were so many decisions to make about what to take and what to leave behind, and this was very hard for both of them. They had had a practice of waiting to buy things until they could buy the best. Now some of these beautiful and functional items would have to be left behind. One valuable piece that was crated to go to Denmark was Mother's Singer treadle sewing machine that could create fancy stitches. Dad had bought it for her early in their marriage, as soon as he could find the means to pay for it. Some books were given away, but most of Dad's books were packed to go with us, as were the silverware, some carpets and an Axminster rug. Clothes for the entire family were carefully prepared.

That summer was very hot and an especially good one for the garden, but we would not be enjoying the produce or the beautiful juicy ripe peaches that were hanging on our tree. There were farewells and tears from time to time. On September 1, we moved in with several families of the congregation. The hard part was yet to come - the auction of our other possessions, including our beloved organ and the mahogany parlor table and chairs. For Dad the hardest of all was leaving Topsy. She had traveled with us to all the congregations that my father served. She was nineteen years old but still spry. After much thought Dad gave her to a very fine farmer, hoping that she would stay with him as long as she lived. Some years later we heard that she had been sold to someone who had not treated her so well. We all felt betrayed. I am sure Topsy felt the same. The day of the auction it was 104 degrees. We had no cool place to rest and sadly watched as our belongings were sold. I can only surmise how my parents must have felt that day. Our comfort came from members of a caring congregation.

Our family left McNabb by train on September 7, 1922, Mother's 46th birthday. Each of us older girls was responsible for one suitcase and one of the younger children. We stayed overnight in the homes of friends and relatives in Chicago. There were too many of us to stay in one place. The next morning we boarded a train for New York. All of us children enjoyed the trip, not really aware of the terrific responsibility such a trip presented for our parents. While the trip was exciting, we were glad when we arrived in New York. Some fellow pastors met us and escorted us to a mission home where the accommodations were simple, but sufficient. I do not recall much about those two days; my heart was still back in Illinois with the friends I had left behind. I do remember that we wondered why we had rashes the next day and then realized that we had become the victims of bedbugs!

A streetcar carried us to the ship. At our destination, only half of the family was able to get off before the streetcar started off again. I was among the group left behind. My twelve-year-old sister Helga was carrying an afghan. Suddenly she yelled, "He is taking the afghan!" When she yelled, the thief got scared and let go. We got off at the next stop, and we were so relieved to find the rest of the family waiting for us there.

Dad gave a sigh of relief when we were finally settled on the ship, which was a Scandinavian liner called *Frederick the Eighth*. Although we were third class passengers, we were given second class accommodations so our sleeping quarters were very comfortable. As we started to sail, I immediately began to feel seasick and ran up to my cabin. As I threw myself on the upper bunk, I took off the burgundy tam-o'-shanter that was popular at the time and which I had crocheted especially for the occasion; grabbing the cap by the pompon I threw it on the porthole ledge, not realizing that the window was open. Out went the cap into the Atlantic Ocean. I ran up on deck to see if I could see it, but it was forever buried in the deep blue sea. Again, I ran up to my cabin saying, "I will never say goodbye again! I will stay put." Little did I know how often in the future I would eat those words!

I was still on the bunk when Dad called us all up on deck. "I want you to see the Statue of Liberty," he said. "You may never have another chance." Crossing the Atlantic Ocean was an unforgettable experience. There were no responsibilities for us, so we just enjoyed spending time with each other. Dad, always the teacher, would tell us about all the sights we saw from the ship, except for the days when all we saw was the majestic Atlantic. Some days were stormy, and we would all have motion sickness. Dad would go around making sure that we were all right. On Sunday, he was asked to lead the worship service on board. After ten days, we passed through the harbor of Christiania (now Oslo), Norway. We arrived in the city early in the morning and left during the evening. The beauty of the sunrise and sunset in the harbor impressed all of us. Our parents, who were both nature-lovers, wanted all of us to appreciate the beauty around us, and we all have been blessed by this teaching.

Greeted with love

We relaxed one more day on board the ship before we arrived in Copenhagen on September 23. One of Dad's brothers was there to greet us and to take us to the home of Dad's oldest sister, Johanne Larsen, where we were greeted with much love. What a reunion and what hospitality we received! Aunt Johanne and Uncle Ditlev owned a large farm - large, that is, according to Danish standards. Denmark is such a small country that land is at a premium; every inch seems put to good use. My aunt and uncle's farm was large enough to give them a good living; they seemed prosperous. The buildings formed a square; the living quarters took up one side, with a beautiful garden in front; the barns and storage sheds formed the other three sides. In the center was a cobblestone courtyard called *gaardsplads*, which was kept very clean. Three of my cousins still lived at home, but Aunt Johanne cleared one large room and set up beds and cots for all of us. After I grew older, I could better appreciate what our relatives had done for us. Since I was accustomed to the hospitality that my parents extended to others, I did not grasp at the time how generous my aunt and uncle were and what a sacrifice it must have been welcoming a family of eleven into their home!

After a few days our family was split: some of us went to Jutland to stay with Mother's family, while the rest stayed with Dad's family. Arrangements were made so that one of us older girls would be with some of the younger ones. I traveled to Langaa where I would stay at Grandma's house. Three of the younger children were with me. I will never forget Mother's reunion with her parents whom she had left nineteen years earlier. As we left the train, Mother walked between her parents, and it seemed that they had completely

17

forgotten that I was there watching out for the other children. It was wonderful to see Mother so happy! Maintaining communication had not been easy during those years apart. There was no telephone service overseas, and letters could take up to three weeks to travel between the two continents. In the intervening years, Mother's brother had died at the age of nineteen, and Dad had lost his mother.

The next six weeks were special as we became acquainted with grandparents, aunts, uncles, and cousins whom we had only known through letters to our parents. We adjusted to our new country quite readily. Over the years in the U.S. we had been told much about Denmark and were encouraged to write to our grandparents in Danish. All of us spoke perfect Danish. We soon felt right at home.

A new country

Home was now a very small country. Denmark is 224 miles long and only about 155 miles wide from Esbjerg on the west coast to Copenhagen. The country consists of the Jutland peninsula, which shares a border with Germany for 42 miles, and about 500 islands, of which only 100 were inhabited at the time we moved there. Although small, Denmark is situated in a strategic location in the midst of great northern European cities, and it became a center for air traffic. One of the differences I first noticed was how crowded the country was compared to the U.S.; the people also were more reserved and more formal in their speech. For example, in interactions with someone who was considered a superior, the people did not call each other by their first names.

Gray, rainy days are typical in Denmark because the country is surrounded by the ocean. In general the temperatures are moderate because of the warming influence of the gulf stream making this climate conducive to beautiful flower gardens which abound. When ice covers the Baltic Sea, however, winters can become quite severe. Denmark is flat and low-lying, and widely cultivated. Dairy and pork products have been widely exported, and Danish fisheries have been among the most important in Europe. Other important industries include the crafting of porcelain, silver products and furniture, engineering, and shipping.

Danes are well educated, and their health care has always been excellent. The government is a constitutional monarchy, meaning that a king or queen is the executive leader but is limited in power by a constitution. Members of the *Rigsdag*, the Danish parliament, are elected by the people. The Evangelical Lutheran Church is the state-supported church of Denmark and is administered by the Ministry of Ecclesiastical Affairs. There is, however, complete freedom of religion in the country.

After six weeks a call came from the government headquarters offering Dad a position in two rural churches in the towns of Simestad and Thestrup. The churches, with a combined total of 1550 members, were situated about three to four miles from each other. They were old - ancient by U.S. standards

- spanning hundreds of years. Dad would serve these two congregations for the next 22 years. A large old parsonage became home and the center of our lives. Here we grew up, entertained, and were sent to school and into jobs.

A door closes

I continued to correspond with George and a couple of his sisters in Illinois. George wanted me to return to the U.S. I loved George but was not prepared to journey to the U.S. unless I would be returning to become his wife. He did not seem ready to make this commitment and did not ask the important question. Then one day I received a letter from George's sister saying that George had met someone else and was planning to marry. I wrote back to her wishing George well. She passed on my good wishes to her brother. He said to her, "It should have been Dagmar; now it's too late." I felt as though a door had closed. I went to my room and gathered all the letters and gifts that he had given me, returned to the living room and one by one, fueled the fire with them. Dad was always adept at getting to the heart of any matter with few words. He acknowledged my behavior with only one sentence, "It appears that it will be very warm in here today."

A door opens

When one door closes, another opens. I had always been interested in nursing; possibly I was influenced by accompanying Dad when he went to visit the sick of the congregation. I stayed with a doctor for a year while I learned clinical skills from him. Encouraged by this work, I applied and was accepted to nursing school. Ten months after I started nursing school at Viborg County Hospital, Marie had the courage to apply and also was accepted. We were the last group of nurses trained in the "old way," which involved learning by doing. Prayer was my constant companion. Over and over I prayed, "Lord, teach me as we go along." The first time I worked in the emergency room, I prayed so hard that an emergency would not come in. By 10:00 A.M., we already had our first emergency! With God's help, all went well.

We were always welcome to bring our friends home with us on our days off. One time Marie and I filled a bus with fellow students who came home for the evening with us and were treated royally by our parents. Dad and Mother loved young people and year after year, they entertained all our friends with food, games, and a time of worship before the guests departed.

My parents' influence continued to guide me during nursing school. One of my nursing supervisors was known to be unreasonably strict and undiplomatic. She was the object of many humorous stories and much gossip in the dormitory. On one of my days off, I was telling Dad about how hard it was to serve on that floor. He said, "Well, it is better there now when you are there. Isn't it?" The stories continued to induce laughter among the students, but

Dagmar as a student nurse in 1929

when I returned, I felt the Lord clearly say to me, "Don't join in that ridicule. Keep your mouth closed." God gave me the grace to find positive things to say about the supervisor. Later when I became her assistant for a year, I learned that she had spent some time in the U.S.A., so we had things in common to share. I also learned that she had been trying to cope with depression. Many years later, when she was 80-years-old, I visited her in her retirement apartment. She now had peace with God, and she thanked me for what I had meant to her. When she was 90, I was home again for a visit and heard that she was in the hospital for the amputation of a second leg. When I went to visit her, I approached quietly since she was very ill. I saw that she had a smile on her face. Surprised, I said, "And you can smile?" "Oh, yes, I can laugh out loud," she replied. Could this be the same stern woman I knew from my nursing school days? What a victory for the Lord!

I graduated from nursing school in 1930 after three years of general training, and then two months of specialty training in obstetrics. Most students received six months of psychiatric training as well. This was waived for me when a doctor told me that I would not need it and asked me to start working in the hospital because there were staff shortages. Marie graduated the follow-

20

Family picture taken in 1930, last time the family was together.
l-r top: Helga, Marie, Bernhard, Richard, Esther,
l-r bottom: Grace, Ruth, Laura, Naomi, Dagmar and Niels Christian

ing year. For a short period of time we worked together at the hospital where we had received our diplomas. Marie excelled in the medical department, while I stayed mostly in the surgical area. No one could beat us in making beds and taking care of our rooms; we had always been a team. During this time Marie, Helga, and I lived in Viborg where we shared a small apartment.

Helga had been only twelve when we moved to Denmark. She was very smart and the first member of the family to be sent to a private school. Although she had received her education in English up to this time, she excelled in her class in Danish! She yearned to go to college and the university, but like Marie and me, she saw that there were many children coming after her who needed financial support. So she took a job in a dentist's office where the dentist trained her to be an excellent technician. Together the three of us started a Bible study group for nurses. All three of us were involved with the Oxford Group Movement, a Christian group led by American, Frank Buchman.

Bernhard's gift

Bernhard was my oldest brother and followed Helga in birth order. He had no desire for higher education and took up the vocation of furniture-making. After we older girls left home, he would come back when Mother needed help and scrub the floors of the parsonage. When he earned his apprenticeship certificate, he became engaged.

21

Bernhard taught us how to die. During his years of apprenticeship, he stayed with a family who had a member with tuberculosis (TB). At 19 years of age he contracted a case of "galloping tuberculosis," as it was called back then, and he was sent to a sanatarium, but nothing helped. The disease attacked all the organs in his body. He was fully aware of his condition. He roomed with two other young men in the sanatarium, and his testimony led one of them to accept Christ. As Christmas drew near, Bernhard begged to be taken home. The doctors, who were touched by his faith and the way he bore his terminal illness, wanted to grant his wish; yet, they were reluctant for him to leave the sanatarium because of the risk of contagion. A public health nurse was sent to the parsonage to see if his needs could be accommodated there. The family all rallied around him. My father moved out of his study, which became Bernhard's bedroom because it was the sunniest room. Marie took a leave of absence from the hospital so that she could care for him.

On Christmas eve, Bernhard was helped into the living room where a floor to ceiling Christmas tree was aglow with candles, or "living lights" as we called them. We maintained our traditional Christmas. Although Bernhard could not partake of the big Christmas dinner, he watched the festivities as we lined up and walked from the dining room to the living room, dancing around the tree and singing as many Christmas carols as we could manage. Next Dad held devotions, reading the scripture and praying and praising God. At ten o'clock that night, Dad said to Bernhard, "We better get you back to bed so you can rest." Ever thankful, Bernhard replied, "Thank you, Dad and Mother. This is the best Christmas I ever had because Jesus is in my heart."

Bernhard had prayed that God would keep his mind clear, and God granted this request to the end. He refused any drug that would sedate him. Gradually his cough got worse. When I had a day off, I would help with his care and stay with him at night. He refused to have any of us sleep in his room, worried that we might become infected. A short time before he died, I was home for the night. I slept on a cot outside his room. There was no sleep for him; he coughed and coughed almost constantly with few breaks. By four o'clock I could not stand it any longer. I went in to him and said, "Bernhard, I wish it was I that was sick and not you." "Oh, Dagmar," he replied, "You must not say that. When I really committed my life to Christ, I prayed, 'Lord if you will save my sweetheart and all my family, I will be willing to die' and then I got sick."

On the 13th of January, we all came home. We called the college requesting officials to tell Richard to come home that afternoon. The family divided into two groups and took turns sitting with Bernhard. He requested that the family talk out loud in his room so he could hear what was being said. Around 8:00 P.M. when Mother and I and two others were sitting with him, he suddenly said, "Shhh! I am going to leave now." We quickly got everyone together and for two hours sat quietly around his bed. Soft drinks were a rare treat at that time; we had bought some since we were doing everything we could think of to please him. He now said, "Dad, remember the soft drink bottles have to be returned." Then he took each of our hands in turn until he had said good-bye to us all. He was perfectly clear as he took each hand and said, "Good night and thank you." When he had spoken with each one of us, he looked up with a shine of glory on his face and began to count. When he had counted to about thirty, Dad said, "What do you see, son?" "I cannot tell you; I wish you knew," he replied. Again he looked up and started counting. Again Dad said, "Can't you tell me a little of what you see?" He gave the same answer, "No, Dad, I can't. I wish you knew!" Then he closed his eyes and was gone. No one seemed to be able to move. I said to Dad, "I have never seen anybody die like this." He quietly said, "Neither have I, but I thought it was because he was our son."

It was a very cold January day when he was laid to rest. The church was packed for the funeral. Pastors from the surrounding areas joined us. The church choir in which Bernhard had sung during his years of apprenticeship sang, "The Great White Host." My father's sermonette began with, "We beheld His glory." After the service one of the pastors said, "I thought we were going to a funeral, but this was a festival." All of us siblings wanted to carry his coffin from the church to the nearby grave site. Another young man helped as well. As we stood by the grave, twelve-year-old Ruth said, "I just can't stand to think of my brother put down there." Then Naomi, who was ten said, "You mustn't think of him down there, but up there," as she pointed upward. Bernhard lives forever in our memories.

Amazing medical technology

I was working contentedly at Viborg County Hospital when I was offered a job as one of seven R.N.s in the country to initially staff the new Niels Steensen Hospital in Copenhagen. This diabetes research center was named after a Danish scientist specializing in the area of diabetes. My supervisor at Viborg Hospital was from the same hometown in Denmark as the doctor of the new hospital, Dr. H.C. Hagedorn. When Dr. Hagedorn offered her the supervisory position at the new hospital, she honored me by asking me to go with her.

That was an exciting time. The 20-bed hospital located in a suburb of Copenhagen opened in 1932 with all the latest technology. The rooms were all single, with hydraulic beds that were raised and lowered by hand. Each had a large wheel that could be manipulated so that the bed could be rolled. When the weather was good, the patients would be wheeled out into the garden. The doctors and nurses went on rounds in beautiful surroundings. One nurse was able to care for both floors at night thanks to the sound system which allowed her to hear everyone at the desk.

Patients' blood sugar was tested four times a day. Until that time, the procedure for testing blood sugar was a lengthy one, but Dr. Hagedorn invented a three-minute method. Staff in the diet kitchen helped patients regulate their blood sugar through their food intake, and before they left the hospital patients were instructed in their diets in the kitchen. Generally patients' blood sugar was regulated, and they were discharged within two weeks.

23

Richard's antics

Richard was one of the more gifted children in our family. We all knew he would go to college. He attended private school and then went to college at Viborg. Initially he did not know what major to take; he talked about becoming an engineer, a doctor, and a pastor. He was in college when Bernhard died. Quite often before his death, Bernhard would ask Richard to come home, and they would have private discussions. I never knew the subject of their talks.

Richard had many friends. There was a group of four young men who were especially full of fun. I was still living in the dormitory at the hospital in Viborg, when one night I returned from work to find the four sitting outside my door, waiting for a snack. From college at Viborg, Richard came to the University of Copenhagen to study theology, so he lived nearby when I worked at the diabetes research center. One night Richard and some of his friends came to see me at my apartment, but Richard could not remember my address. They walked up and down the street, calling, "Dagmar. Dagmar." Somehow we connected!

He found it rather handy to have three older sisters who all were earning a salary. Although I did not have much to offer, I would give Richard a little money when he needed it. As a family what belonged to one belonged to all, and we helped each other get through tough times. I still get a chuckle when I think of him bicycling to my apartment one evening to tell me that he needed some money. I did not question why he needed the money, but I wondered how it had been used. A week later I found out that he and a couple friends had flown to Sweden to get a shave! It was all in fun, but I was a little more careful with my money after that.

Who would have guessed that all four high-spirited friends would become ministers in the Danish church? And who would have guessed that my mischievous brother would one day become a linguist, an interpreter for world-renowned evangelist, Billy Graham, and would spend six years in Sierra Leone after he retired as part of an American-sponsored mission to create a dialogue between the Muslims and Christians?

A variety of nursing duties

It seems as if I was born to start things and move on. This is certainly not what I planned or desired. I would have been happy to stay at the Niels Steensen Hospital, but after 15 months, I developed a back problem. Dr. Hagedorn sent me to Dr. Chievitz who took me off duty and said point blank that I should give up my nursing career. I shed tears and left. When they offered me a sedentary job in the insulin factory, I said, "No thank you."

After being hospitalized for three months for a spinal nerve infection and then recuperating for another three months, I was asked to establish a social nursing program in Simestad where my parents lived. Denmark was one of the leaders at that time in establishing social services. I rode around on my

24

bicycle visiting homes and caring for pregnant women and geriatric patients. I also set up the office and bought needed supplies. After six months in this position, I was once more called back to the hospital in Viborg where I had received my training and first worked as a nurse. The night supervisor who was in charge of five surgical wards was terminally ill, and I was needed. "Oh, Lord," I prayed, "How can I do that?" As I went to my Bible, I stopped at Psalm 127:1. *"Unless the Lord builds the house, its builders labor in vain."* (NIV) In other words if that was the Lord's guidance, I could count on Him. I took over the job as the night supervisor. My heart had always been in two areas of nursing - surgical units and training the young people. Now I was able to do both. Each ward contained 20 to 30 patients with one student nurse providing care. I made rounds, supervised the students and administered all of the meds; I also worked with the doctors in the E.R. I found this job to be very challeng-ing, entailing a great deal of responsibility, and I learned to trust the Lord for guidance in all of my work.

*Dagmar and another missionary at the Dedication Service
for Dagmar when she was being sent to China, 1937*

3

Call to Mission

All authority in heaven and on earth has been given to me. Therefore go and make disciples of all nations, baptizing them in the name of the Father and of the Son and of the Holy Spirit, and teaching them to obey everything I have commanded you. And surely I am with you always, to the very end of the age. Matthew 28:18-20 (NIV).

A seed sprouts

When conditions are right, seeds sown in the minds and hearts of children will sprout and grow. The children in our family were brought up to have a keen knowledge of a loving and caring heavenly Father and a feeling of sincere responsibility to serve Him. No doubt the atmosphere in which I grew up challenged me to think seriously about my responsibility to bring the gospel to those who never had heard it and to share material gifts with the poor. Two experiences further influenced my thinking - the effects of World War I and the experience of interacting with missionaries.

When I was seven and we lived in Michigan, news of the first world war, occuring almost in the backyard of Denmark, became a grave concern for my parents and was often the subject of our daily devotions. Later when we moved to Denmark, post-war problems kept cropping up. Poor children from the south were sent to Denmark, and the organization, Save the Children, was born. Several children spent summer months in our home, and it seemed a natural step for us to want to be part of the healing process.

My parents were mission-minded and frequently invited missionaries who were passing through our area to stay with us. Over the years I had the opportunity to listen to many mission stories and was fascinated by them! I listened to the words of Jesus, *"...Go and make disciples of all nations...," (Matthew 28:19,*

NIV) and thought that I might be a candidate for this role because I had grown up in a pastor's family and was well acquainted with missionaries. As I became older, however, I felt that I was not qualified at all to become a missionary, because I did not think that I was good at approaching people and witnessing. So, I buried this dream in my heart and focussed on my other interest - nursing.

On the surgical ward of the hospital, one of my duties was to care for older men who had undergone prostate surgery. At that time the surgery was a two-part procedure and quite complicated. Since there were no antibiotics to prevent infection, meticulous care was required for recovery. I had been brought up by my parents to be very conscientious, and I also felt responsible to God for my patients' care. One day when I had completed the daily care for three men who had undergone this surgery, one of them turned to me and said, "We want you to be our nurse, if at all possible." They were so thankful for the care they had received. As I went out of that room, it was as if the Lord had said to me, "What are you going to do with this?" And I said, "Well, Lord, my nursing is what I can give you." I did not feel qualified to be an evangelist, but I knew that I was qualified to take care of patients.

Laying a fleece

I was now about 28 years old. It occurred to me that I would not know what the Lord wanted me to do, if I was not open to His plan. I had decided previously that I was not equipped to become a missionary, yet I had not given God a chance to show me His will regarding the issue. So, I decided to "lay out a fleece," as Gideon did:

> *Gideon said to God, "If you will save Israel by my hand as you have promised - look, I will place a wool fleece on the threshing floor. If there is dew only on the fleece and all the ground is dry, then I will know that you will save Israel by my hand, as you said." And that is what happened. Gideon rose early the next day; he squeezed the fleece and wrung out the dew - a bowlful of water. Then Gideon said to God, "Do not be angry with me. Let me make just one more request. Allow me one more test with the fleece. This time make the fleece dry and the ground covered with dew." That night God did so. Only the fleece was dry; all the ground was covered with dew.*
> *Judges 6: 36-40 (NIV)*

I wanted to make certain of God's call to me so I prayed about it and decided on a course of action. The procedure in Denmark was to apply to the Danish Lutheran Mission Board which maintained outreach missions to Africa, China, and India. If an applicant was accepted for service, the board would determine to which of the three locations the applicant would be sent. Several applicants whom I knew applied numerous times until they were accepted. If they were not accepted, they would look for other alternatives and continue to

28

apply. My plan, however, was different. I told the Lord that I would send in one application - only one. If I were not accepted, I would take that as a "No" from God - that I was not to become a missionary. So, I sent in my application.

It took quite a while to hear from the mission board. In the meantime I continued working nights on the surgical wards, and I helped in surgery with young patients who had ear problems. The ear problems were complications resulting from scarlet fever. Soon I also came down with scarlet fever and became quite sick. Since there were no antibiotics to treat this disease, I was placed in a hospital room in isolation for six weeks, during which time I was allowed no visitors. This gave me a lot of time to think and pray about my application to the mission board. I came to view this six weeks as a blessing in disguise. When I was released from the hospital, I felt quite certain that my application would be accepted by the mission board and that I would be sent to China. One night I dreamt that I was traveling by train. On one side of the train I saw mountains and a beautiful lake; on the other side was a river. I remember the dream well because it was so clear to me. This dream was to become very important to me later.

After being released from the hospital, I went to my parents' home to recuperate. My parents were pleased that I had sent my application to the mission board, and they were just as sure as I was that I would be going to China. Their parsonage was located in the country. Mail was delivered by a mailman who rode his bike to their home; he always brought it right into my Dad's office. One day when I was standing there beside Dad's desk, the mailman put an envelope from the Danish Lutheran Mission Board on the desk. I said, "Oh, Dad, I hardly dare open it." He replied, "You go ahead and open it; they have not made a decision by now; I'm quite certain that they would not make such a quick decision." So, I opened the letter. Surprisingly the mission board had made a decision. Their response read, "We are not able to accept you." My answer was a "No"! I looked at my Dad, and he looked at me. I had been so sure that I was going to China. I had to readjust my mind and thinking to that decision and to the fact that becoming a missionary was not God's plan for me.

I returned to my job as head night nurse at Viborg County Hospital. One day in February about three months later as I was resting in my room after a night on duty, there was a knock on my door. The bishop's wife had come to deliver a message. She said, "The board has decided to send you to China and the faster you can go, the better." I wondered what had changed their minds. Later I learned that at the time of my application, the board knew nothing about me; also because Europe was in turmoil, they did not know if they could send out any missionaries, especially to China. Apparently four different board members, however, had come forward and questioned why my application had been denied. "How could you say no to Dagmar?" they asked. My family and I had not told any of the four that I had sent in my application. When they learned about it through other means, they came forward.

One of the four was the Bishop of Viborg. He was my father's bishop and also was acquainted with me from his visits to patients in the hospital. Another board member was a pastor from a neighboring city who knew me personally. The third and fourth board members who came forward knew my parents. One was the general manager at a Christian retreat center where my father and mother had spent a month while my father recuperated following treatment for cancer.

The story of how my parents came to be at that retreat is a special one for my family, and it demonstrates the kindness of the bishop. I had visited my parents on one of my days off and noticed that my father was not feeling well, although he did not complain. I realized that something was seriously wrong and convinced him to go to the doctor. He made an appointment with the head doctor in the hospital where I worked. Soon it was discovered that he had a cancerous tumor by his heart and lungs. He was hospitalized for three months and given radiation treatments. Many prayers were offered on his behalf, and miraculously, he recovered. Sometime after his return to his parish, I could see that he needed to get away because he was extremely tired. He had never taken a vacation, so I wrote a letter to the bishop explaining that my father needed a vacation but that he would never take it on his own and that he could not afford to pay for it. The bishop graciously arranged a wonderful month-long vacation for Mother and Dad at a Christian retreat center with all expenses paid. This meant much to all my family! The general manager of this retreat center was one of the four board members who had come forward on my behalf, even though he did not know me personally.

The timing of the four board members was critical. I became one of four people who comprised the second to the last group of missionaries that the Danish Lutheran Mission Board was able to send to China. There were only two missionaries after our group who were able to get through to China. Later when I was serving in China, I frequently thought back to this unusual experience with the application process. It gave me much needed assurance that indeed God had wanted me to be in China, and it was not a mistake. So, looking back I was glad for the way events unfolded around my application.

Preparing for seven years in China

I now had to prepare for seven years away from home. This involved a lot of work. I resigned from my job at the hospital but worked two more weeks there. I made appointments for physical exams, received a lot of dental care, and prepared the clothes that I would need in China. As a new missionary it was important to be introduced to individuals who supported the work of the missions. We were not expected to raise our own personal support, but we did need to share the goals of the board and become acquainted with people interested in this endeavor. The mission board scheduled speaking engagements for me, and I gave talks to help familiarize people with the project in China. There were many farewell parties for the missionaries who would be leaving; this was one way to raise money for the mission. This was also a way that we found prayer supporters, and I was very glad for my partners in prayer. By the time I left for China I was exhausted from all the work I had undertaken in five months time!

All missionaries sent out by the Danish Lutheran Mission Board were sent for one year to Norway or Scotland for special Bible training. Then they were sent for further training to learn English. This language training was waived for me since I was born and raised in the United States and spoke English as well as Danish. It was felt that in my role as a nurse I also did not need the intensive Bible training required of those being sent as evangelists. I was sent instead for five months of Bible training with a pastor. However, the pastor's wife became ill following the birth of her ninth child, and I spent the time nursing her rather than receiving instruction. I was probably the only missionary sent by the Danish Lutheran Mission Board who did not receive this year of instruction, and I always felt unqualified because I had not received it. I also felt a bit short-changed as it would have been nice to have that year of training to adjust to the thought of being away from my family for seven years and to recover from the months of frantic preparations before the trip. If I had received that year of training, however, I would have missed the opportunity to go to China as no missionaries were allowed into the country later.

"God Be With You 'Til We Meet Again"

In 1937 there was much turmoil in Europe and upheaval in Russia. The years 1937 and 1938 were two of the worst in Russian history. The country was under Stalin's rule, and the people were starving. Stalin's purges were at their zenith, and many victims were being transported to Siberia. I would be traveling by train through Siberia on my way to China. There was confusion about what would be needed for the trip. At first I was told that I would need to take my own food for the nine-day trip. My dear mother was very busy preparing food that I could take along. She conserved chicken and meat in jars that I could open and eat on the way. I was then told that I would not have to take food along for the entire trip; half of the food would be supplied. I left behind some of the food that my mother had worked so hard to prepare.

My father, mother, and 18-year-old sister, Ruth, accompanied me to Copenhagen. It was about a five or six hour train ride. At that time it took longer because there were no bridges across the fjords between the islands, and we had to use ferries, so the trip to Copenhagen took the better part of a day. We stayed overnight at the mission in Copenhagen. The next day I learned that I needed to bring most of my food for the trip after all. At the last minute my family and I rushed out to buy food in Copenhagen that would last me through the trip. It was frustrating for all of us.

It was about 10:00 A.M. on August 6, 1937, when Dad, Mother and Ruth took me to the train station in Copenhagen. Just five months earlier in March we had said good-bye to Marie, who had left to work with Armenian refugees in Greece. Now it was my turn to depart. Four of us missionaries were leaving together that day. One, like me, was a single woman; she had already served two terms in China and was home on furlough. Two were a married couple; they also had been home on furlough after spending one term in China. I was the only first-time missionary who was leaving. Everything was in order; all of our business was taken care of, we had said our good-byes, and we had taken our seats on the train. It was tradition at the time, when a missionary left, that family and friends would gather and sing. Such a group had gathered for the four of us and sang, "God Be With You 'Til We Meet Again."

My eyes were riveted on my Dad's and Mother's faces. "Would I ever see them again?" I wondered. I remember so clearly all the confusing thoughts that were running through my mind. A lot can happen in seven years. Ruth was a healthy 18-year-old so I was sure that I would see her again. As the train rolled out, she ran and ran and ran alongside of it, waving to me. That proved to be the last time I saw her.

Suffering along the Trans-Siberian Railroad

That first day we traveled as far as Berlin, where we stayed overnight. We did some shopping and sight-seeing in the afternoon. Then we changed trains from the European line to the Trans-Siberian Railway. We sat on hard wooden benches which were not very comfortable, and two people shared a cabin. My roommate was Kirstine Moesbaek, the other single missionary.

We went to the dining car for one meal a day. Along the way, we were able to buy eggs. The missionary couple who left Denmark with me were experienced with this and usually obtained eggs for us. Boiling water was available on the platforms of the train stations, so when the train stopped, we were able to step outside for a few minutes, boil our eggs and then eat them inside as our journey continued.

The minute we crossed into Poland from Germany, the mood changed. Poland was already threatened by the Germans at this time. We crossed a bridge on which sentries with their bayonets were stationed. The mood seemed to be one of incredibly heavy suspicion. Nobody smiled. We saw suffering rather than smiles on the faces of the people. In Warsaw we had our first glimpse of total poverty. The people had nothing. Poor homeless people sitting dejectedly jammed the train station. This was our first eye-opener to the poverty of the people and hinted at what they had gone through. It gave us a foretaste of what we would see and experience in the years to come.

Another image made a deep impression on me. A boy was standing at one of the train stations in Russia. He appeared to be about 12 to 14 years old. I suppose he had lost everything. His eyes seemed to be saying, "Have you something? Can you give me something?"

It was common during trips by train for travelers to throw their soiled clothing out the window. If we had clothes which needed washing that we did not want to take with us, out it went! Anything that was thrown out, including underwear that had been worn, was snatched up by the local people as if it were priceless.

An intourist man was assigned to all people traveling through Russia and Siberia. Travelers were told that the intourist man would protect them, and we were told to go to him if we had any problems. In actuality, the government was suspicious of everyone. We were traveling during the cruel period when Nikolai Ivanovich Yezhov was head of the Secret Police and during the time of Stalin's great purge when thousands of people were uprooted from their homes and moved to Siberia. All travelers were thus under constant surveillance. If need be, an intourist man would keep us in line.

Most of the others passengers on the train were Russians. We were not able to talk with them. There was the language barrier, and we could not trust each other. There was one elderly gentleman with a long beard, however, who caught our eye. We realized from some subtle gestures he made that he was a Christian; we felt a bond with him. Many white Russians fled to Manchuria during those years.

We stopped in Moscow and were allowed to do some sight-seeing with an escort. We were told to make ourselves look as plain as possible. We were to wear no stockings and definitely no jewelry. The masses of people were desperately poor and without items in life that we might think basic. If we looked too bourgeois, we might be attacked. Even though we tried to look plain, we were the object of obscene words and gestures as we sat on a park bench. The people had been so indoctrinated with communist propaganda that anyone who was perceived to have something of value was hated. It was a reaction against the days when the czar and the elite of Russia lived in luxury while the peasants received nothing for their toil and lived in dire poverty.

As our train traveled through Russia, we saw trainload after trainload of boxcars jammed with hungry, despairing people headed for Siberia. We could see them standing in front of the open doors to the boxcars. We felt so helpless. We were not free to talk with anybody, and we knew that if they talked with us they could be killed. The misery of the people broke our hearts. There we were for nine days, cooped up in our train, looking through the window at all of the suffering and destruction. The experience left a terrific impression on us - one that we would never get over.

God's assurance

In some locations the beautiful countryside was encouraging to us. We were traveling in August so it was very warm, and at one point we saw miles and miles of beautiful white birch trees. This was unusual to see on the journey, since many of the trees had been cut down. Toward the end of our trip through Russia, we went past Lake Baikal, the largest freshwater lake in Eurasia and the deepest lake in the world. It is up to 50 miles in width and stretches for almost 400 miles between mountains rich in mineral resources. The lake contains numerous species of fish, many of them unusual. The beautiful view was familiar as I gazed at it. Then it dawned on me that this was the very scene that

I had seen in my dream when I had been recuperating in the hospital from scarlet fever! This realization provided me with further assurance that my trip to China was God's plan for me.

4

China Mission

The Lord will guide you always; he will satisfy your needs in a sun-scorched land and will strengthen your frame. You will be like a well-watered garden, like a spring whose waters never fail. Isaiah 58:11 (NIV).

Introduction to a foreign culture

When the train came close to Irkutsk near the Chinese border, all the shades were pulled down on the windows. We were not allowed to see anything, and the border was patrolled. Much of the civil war between the red and white Russians had been fought in this area. A similar civil war was erupting in China.

Our trans-continental journey ended as the train pulled into Harbin located in Manchukuo (Manchuria). Manchuria is in the northeastern part of China; at the time I was there it was considered a separate entity from China. I would be conducting all of my work with the Chinese people in Manchuria, and we planned to stay for a short time at our Danish mission in Harbin. The few Danish missionaries stationed there worked with the local women and maintained a church.

It was August and very hot. The people and landscape seemed familiar to me from looking at photographs and pictures in mission magazines. The Chinese people were squatting or stooping in their fields. They were almost hidden under their large cone-shaped straw hats, which they tied under their chins as protection from the sun. The constant noise and Chinese music, however, were foreign to me, and during that first long, hot summer night, I wondered if I ever could become accustomed to these sounds.

Teachers at the College of Chinese Studies in Peking

Harbin was just a brief layover for me. I soon boarded one of the rather new and fine Japanese express trains that took me south through Manchuria to Antung, situated near the Korean border. Well-dressed uniformed personnel served the passengers. For the first time in all my travels, I experienced the luxury of being handed, via tongs, a hot damp wash cloth, to wipe away dust and perspiration before a meal was served. On the train the only reminders of the war were the many Japanese military personnel who were headed south after their invasion and occupation of Manchuria.

I stayed the last week in August in Antung and became acquainted with Karen Gormsen and other Danish missionaries stationed there. Antung was one of the largest - if not the largest - Danish mission stations in China. It consisted of men's and women's hospitals, an orphanage, a church, and a school

36

for missionary children that was quite new. A few miles away a new theological seminary had just been built. The Olsens, a Danish family who served the agricultural department, lived there. Johanne Olsen and Margrethe Aagard Poulsen, who were both nurses, had established a large mission outreach. Margrethe came down with typhus after caring for patients. She later died and was buried in a beautiful spot on a cold blustery winter day in December, 1944.

Gerda Beck, another Danish nurse who had arrived in China shortly after me, and I next went to Peking (now Beijing) where we attended the College of Chinese Studies. The college was an American institution where missionaries and business people alike learned the Chinese language. Gerda and I joined a group of young English and American missionaries for our studies, and we were fortunate to have some very experienced Chinese teachers who had taught many foreigners throughout the years. Our favorite teacher was known as "Dearest." We also always called him by that name. Our second favorite was "Tiger." There were other good teachers as well. We were expected to speak only Chinese on the campus; this helped facilitate our learning. Dearest taught by telling many stories. One day he told us the story of a former student who had scurried out into an icy road in winter literally running into one of his teachers who fell down on his behind. Totally embarrassed, the student said, "*Ching tsoa pa; ching tsoa pa*," meaning, "Please sit down; please sit down." What he had wanted to say was, "Excuse me; excuse me!" Needless to say, the class learned these words well.

During our free time we toured the temples and nearby mountains, the Forbidden City, the Great Wall, the summer palace, and other interesting places. We also enjoyed games of volleyball and friendship gatherings. On Sundays we attended church services in the city, following the language as well as we could by taking our Bibles with us. We listened to the now famous Wang Ming Tao. At the time we had no idea that we were listening to a young man who was to become an important spiritual leader, one who would later pay the price of torture and imprisonment for his faithfulness to his Lord.

It was during this time that I first met and visited Rosalind Rinker, a beautiful American Christian who worked with Intervarsity Christian Fellowship. Many years later she visited the University of Wisconsin-Madison campus and my home, which was about 30 miles from Madison. During the visit she gave me her well known book on prayer.

It was a very productive year which ended too early for us because of the Japanese hostilities and expansionistic policies. Gerda Beck and I left in the spring for our own mission stations. Gerda was sent to Feng Hwang Cheng situated north of Antung; I was sent to Suiyen which is northeast of Antung. The Suiyen mission compound consisted of a hospital, a church, and missionary homes. Built in a valley, surrounded on all sides by mountains and protected by the usual wall, it was in a sense a sheltered place. In this beautiful place, however, I was also introduced to atrocities that were foreign to me and which gave me the initial shocks of barbarism. Decapitated heads were hung on posts outside villages to coerce people into submission. The horrifying practice could have been done at this time by either the Japanese or the Chinese police, both of whom disregarded human rights. One day I saw some trucks go by laden with Chinese people. Shortly afterward I heard shots ring out. I learned later that 40 people had been rounded up, driven into the countryside, lined up by a ditch, and shot one by one. The bodies were left in the ditch. Throughout that winter, body parts, dragged around by dogs, were often deposited on mission property.

"The Lord will guide you always"

The medical department at Suiyen consisted of three doctors and a nurse. The nurse, Helga Johansen, who was about my age, died of typhus during my stay in China. Her body was carried by her staff of young people up the mountain where she was buried. Three other female missionaries served the local Chinese women. This was the setting in which I first ventured out to try my language skills and to try to witness for Jesus. I learned several very important lessons. The first and most important was that I had nothing to offer without the Lord. Looking back over those years in China, I see clearly, what I then learned experientially. We missionaries worked under a huge canopy of prayers from our families, our friends, and other wonderful people who supported the missions. In times of stress, danger and war, people tend to pray more strategically, i.e., they can be very specific about what to pray for when there is grave danger. When we could get news to our prayer partners at home, we were protected by their entreaties to the Lord. We often commented, "Someone prayed for me today," when we had triumphed over seemingly insurmountable difficulties.

I had a wonderful view from the window in my little second story room. One morning, a feeling of inferiority nearly overwhelmed me as I thought of the tasks ahead. I was reading Chapter 58 of Isaiah. When I read verse 11, *"The Lord will guide you always"* (NIV), I seemed to see Jesus sitting on an empty chair by the window. Whether this was a vision or a figment of my imagination, it was vivid enough to become a promise to me throughout my life.

With this promise of continual support and guidance, I began to talk to the young student nurses and sometimes the patients. One young male patient, who was about 20 years old, was terminally ill. I spoke to him as carefully as I could and ended up telling him to talk to God. "Oh!" he whispered, "I can't pray." He meant that he could not talk. I then explained to him that he did not have to say the words aloud; he could just talk to the Lord in his heart. Later that night Helga went to see him, and he whispered to her, "Pray for me." She did so. Then he was moved to a single room. His father came to be with him. Helga later told me that when he died a light surrounded him, and his father asked to become a Christian.

One late afternoon I was sitting by my desk when our houseboy came to get my lamp to fill with kerosene. One of his jobs was to see that all the lamps were ready when needed. As he left, a "voice" seemed to say to me, "Give him $2.00 (a yen)." Well, I thought wryly, why not give him $3.00? That is all the money I had. The urge came back, "Give him $2.00." The houseboy came back with a clean lamp, and I gave him the money. He looked surprised, said, "*Hsieh. Hsieh* (Thank you. Thank you.)," and left. A few days later I heard from Helga that he had told her about the wonderful way in which God had helped him. He had been summoned to the Yamen (the police headquarters) where he was told that he must pay a fee of $2.00 for the burial of his father. He had not known what to do since he did not have the money. That very day I had given him the $2.00 that he so desperately needed.

On occasion there were joyful days, ones in which we could enjoy the beauty of the environment and focus on our goal of bringing the gospel story to those who had never heard it. On one such day a young visiting missionary and I climbed one of the beautiful mountains armed with our Bibles, pads of paper, pencils, and a lunch. In this glorious setting we developed a plan to help the young Chinese Christian girls remain active in their prayer lives. We wrote out a prayer list, suggestions for each day of the week, to guide the young converts as they began to pray.

Vacations in Korea

Twice I had the privilege of spending about a week with a small group of missionaries in Pyong Yang, Korea, which is now North Korea. A family of Presbyterian missionaries, the Underwoods, had built a resort for fellow missionaries. In this setting I could really relax, and I had an opportunity to become acquainted with people from other religious denominations. On Sundays and other occasions we would meet at "The Point" where a natural amphitheater was created around the inlet of the bay. On a Sunday evening during my second vacation in this setting, I was asked to lead the service for our group of 10 to 12 American and European missionaries. I recall choosing Psalm 147:1, *"How good it is to sing praises to our God" (NIV)*. We felt blessed by our fellowship, praising the Lord. Shortly after we departed for the night, someone knocked on our door. We were given orders by Japanese authorities that we were all to pack up immediately and take the train back to Manchuria the next morning. That was the end of our vacations at the resort in Korea.

Luggage and clothing were thoroughly searched before passengers were allowed on the train in Korea. After all belongings had been ransacked, we were escorted to the train, and the train was sealed. I was fortunate to have a good seat for the two-day trip. I was so weary and felt so worn out that I said to the Lord, "Lord, I am unable to take over my future responsibilities if I do not get some rest and feel better." It seemed that the Lord just put me to sleep. I slept soundly for hours while the train traveled north. When I arrived, I felt refreshed and ready to go to work. But first, I would face another harrowing experience.

From the Korean border, I traveled alone back to my mission station in

Manchuria. As I tried to board the train in Hsin Ching, the station was so filled with people that it was impossible to move. I became tired after standing and holding my small suitcase for such a long time. I put my suitcase on the floor right behind me and then was pushed backward by people who were jostling to get on the train platform. The only thing I could do was to call out to the Lord for help. I was pushed back up, and I quickly grabbed my suitcase. I had never before had to fight for survival in an unruly crowd, and I hope never to be in such straits again. Twelve people were trampled to death that day.

Ministering to patients

I was sent late in the summer of 1939 to Sweihuafu to substitute for a month in our northernmost hospital and mission station while Anna B. Nielsen, another Danish missionary, was on summer vacation. My nursing skills had not been exercised for a long time. I found it quite difficult to handle this on-again, off-again nursing responsibility. This month it was even more difficult because I worked with a Danish American doctor. I found that American medical terms were different from our Danish ones. Also, I was still studying the Chinese language and had a long way to go. It was one thing to use the vocabulary I had mastered, but it was quite another to understand everything my patients reported. Fortunately, Chinese nurses were always on hand to help me, and God did not let me down when I trusted Him for guidance.

As I went on my rounds of the men's ward one day, my attention was drawn to a nice-looking young man who had been brought in from a remote area. He was very quiet. I did not talk with him, but for some reason I could not get him out of my mind. I felt that I should get him a Chinese Bible. I always had some on hand, but now I had only one left. As I arrived home that day, I wondered whether I should give away the last Bible I had available. I still felt the urge to give it to the young man; so, I hurried back to the hospital to give it to him. Tears came into his eyes as I handed him the Bible. Using a nurse as an interpreter, he told me that he had been praying for one. He had not been able to bring his to the hospital because he had left home so fast.

Another patient on my rounds was a young girl who was lying in a ward with six other women. The girl was experiencing great abdominal pain. The doctor had ordered hot "stoops." I had not heard the term "stoops" before, but I understood that he wanted me to keep the hot, wet compresses on her abdomen. Even though I did this, the pain remained intense. I did not know her diagnosis, but no surgical procedure was ordered. As I went on my evening rounds, she was still in pain. I stood by her bedside. It was then that the Lord nudged me to pray for her. However, the thought immediately came to my mind, "Suppose that prayer does not help. How will that affect the other women in the room who do not know Jesus?" Again, I felt the urge to pray for her. I tried to make her comfortable and then, with all seven women listening, I prayed as well as my limited language allowed before I left for the night. Many times during that night I prayed for her and pleaded with Jesus to heal her. I rushed to her room the next morning and found her smiling. All the pain was gone and she was on the road to recovery! I was one thankful person! How often Jesus said, *"Oh, you of little faith"* (Matthew 6:30, NIV). I was one of these of whom He spoke. A year later I was again in this mission station substituting during Anna's vacation. I learned that the girl who had been in so much pain had become a Christian and had asked to be baptized.

A child's faith

I moved again in the fall of 1939. The war had intensified; missionaries who were home on furlough were not returning to China. I was becoming aware that my role was to be a fill-in for all types of work. This was fine with me, as I learned a lot from these many experiences. I moved to Fu Yu, our most western mission station. The Fu Yu compound consisted of a church, accommodations for a mission family who were now in Denmark, and a house for two women missionaries. I was sent to be a companion for Inger Almstock, who was now alone in this far-out station which was close to the Gobi Desert of Mongolia. The plan was for me to continue my language studies. (I had already flown to Dairen once in a very small Japanese plane to complete my first year language exam). I learned much from my new co-worker, and Inger had a delightful sense of humor. I was glad to share the work and a home with her.

As always, we witnessed practices that assaulted our sensibilities. My new home was in a dreary dull town of mud houses and walls. Everything seemed to be the same brown color. I had arrived during a time of drought, and Gobi sand seeped through doors and windows and into cupboards and drawers. Worst of all, we watched with horror the heathen practices of trying to appease the gods as people begged for rain. In the very cold winter, the bodies of children who had died would be thrown to the dogs and the corpses dragged around to appease the angry gods. Yet God's love reached past the heathen practices to many of the local people. One day I was sitting at my desk working with the Chinese characters while Inger was out among the people doing the work of the mission. A young girl named Wu knocked on my door. When I called, *"Ching laipa"* (Come in), she came just inside the door and stood looking shyly at the floor. She urgently blurted out one short sentence that got right to the point of her visit, "I am baptized, but I am not saved." I was able to explain to her how Jesus forgave her all her sins and that if she confessed and accepted His forgiveness, she would be saved. We knelt down together and prayed. She arose with peace and also with fire for the Lord in her heart. Soon she brought all four of her sisters to Christ!

One day Wu arrived and asked me to accompany her to visit a friend who was very ill. I went with her and was introduced to the friend's mother; the mother, however, did not welcome me. I asked her if we could pray for her daughter but received no answer. I told Wu that we would pray for her friend on our own. Around that time I received several letters from the young girls in

Chinese young people with Dagmar

Suiyen telling me stories about their new-found faith. I invited Wu to go with me and to encourage her friend to read these letters in her native language from girls her own age. I again tried to explain to the friend's mother about God's love and care. I described how God answers prayer but that sometimes we ask for things that are ultimately not in our best interest. God, knowing what is best for us, answers differently than how we expect at times. I used a metaphor of a bottle of poison. I explained that if a mother had a small child who asked for the poison, the mother would say , "No," because it would be harmful to the child. God gives His children of all ages things that are good. I prayed for Wu's friend before leaving. Some time later Wu told me that this event changed the mother's attitude entirely. The mother had been contemplating giving her daughter poison to end her life. God had guided me to choose a story that spoke directly to the mother as no other illustration could. Wu's friend became a believer.

A sigh speaks when words cannot

So, during those difficult years, the Lord worked. I often thought of a sincere Christian woman in Denmark who once said to me about herself, "The Lord must be very hard up for workers, when He uses me!" I certainly could relate to her sentiments.

Inger and I celebrated a very simple, lonely Christmas that year. Just the two of us sat in front of a little tree trimmed with "living lights." As the last candle burned out, Inger gave a big sigh that expressed so much.

5

Hardships Under the Japanese

In all the travels of the Israelites, whenever the cloud lifted from above the tabernacle, they would set out; but if the cloud did not lift, they did not set out - until the day it lifted. Exodus 40:36-37 (NIV).

Protected by canopies

As I reflect back on the years I spent in China, I realize that the younger missionaries such as I were protected by two canopies. The first was the canopy of prayer provided by our families, friends, and other supporters; the second was protection provided by the older, more experienced missionaries. The Danish missionaries who had come before us built 14 churches, three hospitals, two orphanages, several schools, and had created the mission compounds. Our work was made easier because these institutions had already been established. The more experienced missionaries also came forward to take the brunt of the many police questionings to which we now were subjected. It was imperative that identical answers be given to officials each time they asked their multitude of questions. One Chinese friend described life this way, "The laws are made to be broken;" they were impossible to live by. The Japanese had created these laws to entrap the Chinese and to thus rid the country of all Chinese leadership.

Pastors under duress

In April, 1940 we learned that Hitler had invaded Denmark. Concerned about how the Chinese church could be sustained without Danish financial support, we were happily surprised to see the Chinese Christians courageously

43

take over. While country after country fell under fascist and nazi rule, Japan was feverishly sending troops into China. Food was restricted, but we knew that God would give us our daily bread - one day at a time. Travel was limited to two or three days a month, for example the 11th and 21st days of each month, enabling the Japanese to maintain better control. Under these circumstances it became increasingly difficult for the men in our mission. Since men headed the mission stations at that time, the Japanese considered them dangerous people. They were afraid of the influence that the Danes might have over the Chinese. The men were thus the first people to be denied the right of traveling freely. The Danes were careful to comply. They needed to be cautious in order not to do anything that would endanger the lives of the Chinese to whom they were ministering.

In the spring of 1940 I was transferred again, this time to Hsin Ching, located in the central part of Manchuria. Hsin Ching was the capital of Manchuria; it was where the last Emperor resided. The Emperor was in residence while I was there. If we walked close to his palace, which was more prison than palace to him, we could see the guards lined up on both sides of the street. Security police were all around.

Inside the mission compound walls where we lived were the women's quarters. This consisted of living space for three Bible Women, Chinese Christians who helped to spread the gospel, a room where the local Chinese women came for instruction in preparation for baptism and where they could reside for a period of time while they received this instruction, a residence for a missionary family, and a little house for a single missionary. The little house had been furnished by the previous female missionary, who was now home on furlough and unable to return. This became my home for most of the next four years.

During the first few years in Hsin Ching, I lived next to the Frimer-Larsen family. They became very dear friends of mine. They had four lovely children - a twelve-year-old boy, a ten-year-old girl, a four-year-old girl, and a little boy less than a year old. I became the little boy's Godmother. It was so good to have them close.

The responsibilities that were on the shoulders of the Danish pastors who provided support to the Chinese pastors became very heavy. New edicts came from the Japanese authorities which tried to force the Chinese churches to conduct a ceremonial ritual of bowing to a picture of the Japanese sun goddess Shinto before each service. At one point all the Chinese pastors from Manchuria were called to a conference in which they were required to bow to the sun goddess. Those who did not bow would be under surveillance. I will never forget the meeting of these dear pastors in the Rev. Frimer-Larsen's home after that conference. The pastors called out to the Lord for grace to continue to lead their congregations. Some interpreted the ritual only as a national courtesy, while others considered compliance as breaking God's commandment, *"Thou shalt have no other gods before me."* This caused division among church leaders. The churches which refused to bow before the picture were forced by the Japanese to close.

On my own

Before the edict was enforced, Pastor Frimer-Larsen became ill, and the family was forced to leave. He was taken to our northernmost hospital. He later journeyed back to Denmark where he died soon afterwards. Now I was the only Dane in the city, and I did not know of any other Europeans there. While I initially wondered what I could do alone, I realized that I still could work with the Chinese pastor and the Bible Women. Every day after morning devotions the Bible Women came to me to report on their work and to study the Bible. These were very special times.

During this time I met with new challenges at my mission station. The Japanese often hindered the Chinese pastors in doing their work, so the pastors called on me for help. As a woman, I could still go into the village with our Bible Women to visit the Christian families. Often they would ask me to see some of their friends. On one such occasion we visited a very sick woman who had some open sores on her body. The family was very thankful that we had come and wanted to serve us hot tea. The sick woman was lying on a warm *kang*. The *kang* was the main part of a Chinese home. It was like a stage built in the house adjacent to the kitchen. It was about three feet high with flues attached underneath. Heat from a huge iron cooking kettle would be directed into the flues under the *kang*. This kept the *kang* warm and comfortable for the family who slept on it at night and lived on it in the daytime. A clothesline was stretched above the woman. Flies were buzzing all around. Another woman took a dirty towel from the line and wiped a cup well before pouring tea for me. I had not yet forgotten my sterile "surgical procedures" that were ingrained in me from nursing practice, but I sent a prayer heavenward for my continued health and graciously thanked her for the tea, knowing that if I did not accept it, I would truly hurt her feelings. It was so important to remember that we were ambassadors for Christ under all circumstances.

We continued to carry out our mission work under continuous surveillance and obstacles. Besides holding Sunday School in the city, we taught classes in a little farmhouse a mile or so out in the country. We brought with us teaching aids such as song books and posters depicting Bible stories. One summer day when I walked with two of the Bible Women to the farmhouse, we were stopped about half way there by the Japanese police. They wanted to know where we were going and why, and what we carried in our briefcase. One of my Chinese companions talked while I prayed silently, and for some reason they let us go on our way one more time. As we came closer to the farmhouse, we were greeted by a large group of children standing on a mound watching for us. We were welcomed with cheers and led into a family's small living area where 80 children stood crowded together eager to hear stories about Jesus! That was the last day we were allowed to go there. Years later it still hurts to think about this premature end to such an important ministry.

Another day I walked to the repair shop in the city carrying my broken suitcase. On the way I stopped in a department store to buy some small items.

Dagmar, left, with co-workers at an orphanage

When I had walked halfway home, I was again stopped by the police. They insisted that I had shoplifted some items. All I could do was pray. I was alone and in the hands of brutal people. Then my fear seemed to evaporate. I sensed that God had sent protection. After being detained for far too long, I was finally released. Later there were reports that a Russian woman had taken some items from a store without paying for them. Only God knows how I escaped unharmed from such incidents over and over again.

Hunger, suspicion, and uncertainty

Life was very hard for the Chinese during the winter of 1941. The Japanese used Manchuria to store and supply food for the army, so there was little left for the local people. We would stand in line for hours for a loaf of bread, but somehow we always had food. A Christian Japanese pastor and his lovely family lived in the city and helped us as much as they could. We thanked God for them.

The Chinese had very meager meals. One day when one of the Bible Women came back from her visit to an outlying village, she told of an incident that she had witnessed. A little Chinese woman had somehow acquired a small bag of rice. The police knocked it out of her hand and scattered it in the dirt. Patiently she got on her knees and picked up every grain only to suffer the same insult once again. Again, she gathered her precious rice. Then the police questioned why she had the rice since it was not allowed. She responded that it was for her sick child. This is just one example of the many hardships that the Chinese endured.

Before December 7, 1941, when Pearl Harbor was bombed and America entered the war, a young American man found his way up to the Manchurian capitol, evidently to find out how we were faring. He did not visit me, yet when he left the city, I woke up one day to find policemen on all four sides of our compound making it next to impossible for me to leave the compound for two days and nights. I imagine that the Japanese wondered why the man, who had been so naive in coming to visit us, had been there as they were always suspicious of foreigners.

As the Pearl Harbor attack caught Americans by surprise, it also brought dramatic changes to the missionaries who were stationed in Manchuria. The English and Americans were forced to leave their work, some of them were interned, some were jailed, and some were fortunate enough to get home prior to that history-making day. Some of the Danish missionaries who had lived in China for many years packed up and returned to Denmark. Those of us who were left lived with a great deal of uncertainty, not knowing from day to day what would happen to us.

Under the cloud

I had a siege of stomach trouble during this time and found myself hundreds of miles from any of the three mission hospitals. I wrote to our doctor in Suiyen, the mission station where I had first served. She advised me to obtain permission to travel to the station to be treated. Acquiring such a permit was a major effort which involved a rickshaw ride across the city to the Japanese

Manchurian headquarters. A permit was issued so that I could be gone for two weeks, but I was not allowed to determine when to go or return. We received permission to travel only three days a month, and we were under continual surveillance.

The trip to Suiyen took two days by train and bus. These vehicles were filled to a capacity that is beyond belief unless seen by your own eyes. After my physical examination, the doctor advised me to have my permit extended by a couple months so that I could be treated in the hospital. I prayed about this for a few days and then felt led to go to the police headquarters to apply for an extended permit. My request for the permit was refused, and I was told to go back to Hsin Ching when my two weeks were up. I wondered how I could be so sure that God wanted me to stay when the Japanese authorities denied me the permit. I had no choice. As always, I read the scriptures and prayed until I found peace in my decision. One morning I read Numbers 9:21-23:

Sometimes the cloud stayed only from evening till morning, and when it lifted in the morning, they set out. Whether by day or by night, whenever the cloud lifted, they set out. Whether the cloud stayed over the tabernacle for two days or a month or a year, the Israelites would remain in camp and not set out; but when it lifted, they would set out. At the Lord's command they encamped, and at the Lords's command they set out. They obeyed the Lord's order, in accordance with his command through Moses. (NIV)

The passages came alive as if they had been written just for me in the year 1942. Now I knew that I should leave and not question God's guidance.

My journey back was lonely, tedious, and strenuous. The buses were in poor condition, and there were no motels or rest rooms along the way. When I arrived back in Hsin Ching, I was almost immediately greeted by two Korean policemen who often came to my home. (Many Koreans lived in Manchuria at that time. Both Chinese and Koreans were expected to serve in Japanese government jobs.) The policemen wanted to know why I had returned so early because they had told me that I could have an extension if I needed it. After I told them that the police in Suiyen would not issue a permit, they said, "We advise you to get an extended permit from the headquarters here immediately and go back." I was very puzzled. Then one of them asked, "Why have you, a single woman, come here and stayed through this time?" I told them how I had come to share news about God's love for all people. One replied quietly, "When this war is over, we want you to come back and tell us some more."

The day I came back a young Chinese girl, whom I had known for a short time, came to see me. The girl had come to the mission station because she was afraid of her stepmother. The girl was the oldest of several children. Her mother had died, and her father had remarried a girl about her own age who had tried to kill her. While she was living at the mission, she had become a Christian. She told me that her brother had arranged a marriage for her, and

Chinese young people Dagmar worked with

the man she was compelled to marry was not a Christian. She was not able to refuse to marry the man, but had been praying that I would return and be with her when she was married. That was the only way she could tolerate going through with the marriage. When she saw that I had returned, she realized her prayers were answered.

Once again I hired a rickshaw to go across the city to the police headquarters. Along the way I felt a strong urge to stop and see a very wealthy family whose mother and beautiful daughters were Christians. I had been asked to go to their home to teach the girls piano lessons because they were not allowed to go to the mission station. I almost resisted the urge to stop because I knew this family had no material needs while so many others needed me more. The urge to stop persisted, and I realized that God wanted me to follow it. Mrs. Wang greeted me at the door looking sad. When I asked her how her family was doing, she responded, "Did you not know that Wu Wen is dying?" I had not known this sad news and asked to see her. As Mrs. Wang led me through their beautiful home, I saw the family gathered in the dining room looking very sad. They had tried all the doctors and various remedies available to them, but Wu Wen's condition continued to worsen. She had typhus and had bled profusely. I found Wu Wen unconscious on her bed. She was unresponsive and waxy pale; I could hardly feel a pulse. I knelt down by her bed and prayed for her. Mrs. Wang then asked me to go back to the mission and see if the Chinese pastor and a Bible Woman would come the next day at ten o'clock

49

to baptize her daughter. Before I returned to the mission, I continued on my way to the police headquarters to get my permit renewed; this was accomplished without much delay.

The next day we gathered to pray and to baptize the twelve-year-old girl. She was still unconscious and was baptized without knowing it. We took turns staying with her and praying with the family in the dining room. At approximately four o'clock that afternoon, I was with Wu Wen; there still had been no change in her condition. Her fourteen-year-old sister came in to be with me. She brought with her a silver cross on a chain that she had ordered made for her sister. As I looked on, she took the cross, held it over her sister's head, and lowered it before her face. Suddenly sweat broke out on Wu Wen's forehead, her cheeks turned pink, and she opened her beautiful black eyes. We called in the rest of the group to witness the change in her condition. Her father, who was not a believer, grabbed his brother around the waist and danced around the room saying, "Wu Wen is living. Wu Wen is living." What joy we all experienced that day! Daily, while I was still in the city, I went to the home to help Wu Wen understand a little more about the meaning of her baptism. One day she put her little hand under her pillow and pulled out a ten yen bill. She asked me to give the money to the church, and she wanted to get up and go to church to tell everyone what Jesus had done for her.

Shortly afterwards the Japanese pastor came to see me. He told me that he had been to the police station and had heard that a warrant had been issued for my arrest. I had been accused of bribery to get a permit! The pastor told the authorities that he knew me very well and that I was not capable of such action. I never heard any more about it.

Two weeks later I was back in the interior for treatment of my stomach condition. The two months of medical leave passed very quietly and quickly. The mission station where I received treatment was the same station where I had spent my first year in China studying the language. While I rested under the doctor's care, I spent some refreshing time with fellow missionaries. I had learned not to question the movement of the cloud in my life.

Prayers for new friends and family

During December, 1941, we were planning for the Christmas celebration. So many children came to Sunday School, that we were holding sessions on Thursdays also. The Chinese pastor came to me and asked if I would go for a week to help out in a city north of us where a Chinese evangelist and several Bible Women were working. I replied that I was needed for the continuing work in our station and was especially busy because of the upcoming Christmas celebration. When the pastor asked me a second and then a third time, I knew I had to go. One of the Bible Women and I got ready and traveled an hour north by train.

The young evangelist was so happy that I came that it warmed my heart. I was installed on the *kang* in a little room just off the chapel. The chapel was a rather small room with crude benches and a small charcoal stove in the middle. I held meetings there every day. This was my first experience in conducting meetings over a several day period in Chinese. After our evening meeting the young people would come into my room asking to learn more about the country of the missionaries. We chatted and became acquainted with each other. I planned to have the last meeting with them on Dec. 22, but they begged me to stay one more day. I still felt the need to get back to my home base to help with Christmas preparations, but I could not refuse them. After the evening meeting the young women wanted to come into my room and chat one last time. I told them that I would be there to pray with all who wanted to give their hearts to Jesus. I went into my little room, and for three hours I was on my knees with one after the other who wanted to follow Jesus!

Every night I prayed for all my family. That night I named them one by one, and prayed, "Lord, I have no way of knowing if they all are still alive, but until I know, I will pray for each one." I found out five months later that my sister Ruth had died that night at the age of 23.

A few months later the Bible Woman again went up to the city where the evangelist ministered. She came back with the good news that two of the women who had surrendered to Christ had been baptized earlier. They were both midwives. Now they rededicated their lives to Christ and opened their homes so that Christian meetings could continue. How thankful I was that I had gone to them even though I had wanted to stay in the mission station. It proved to be my last opportunity to visit that city, because that winter a terrible epidemic of the Black Plague, which is carried by rats, broke out in several cities including that one. Many sections of the city were burned to the ground to prevent the spread of the disease. Our mission compound in Hsin Ching was spared.

When duty conflicts with duty

News regarding what was happening in China was very scarce. One of the Danish pastors somehow managed to listen to a shortwave radio at night. He faithfully sent out a bulletin to each mission station whenever possible. The war was pushed into high gear. Supplies diminished for civilians. Chinese soldiers were conscripted, and spying increased. The missionaries were all becoming exhausted, and we suffered also as extreme pressure was exerted upon our dear Chinese co-workers and fellow believers. The missionaries who were left began to gather in Antung near the Korean border. Each of us had a suitcase packed with our most important belongings, so we could leave on short notice. In the fall of 1943 I also said good-bye to my dear co-workers in Hsin Ching and left for Antung.

In Antung I was given a couple rooms in the mission orphanage. One of the most difficult decisions I was called upon to make was whether I would help out in the orphanage or the hospital. I consulted Dr. Pedersen about my dilemma. He responded, "It is hard to decide when duty conflicts with duty." I knew that I could best serve in the hospital because of my nursing background,

The hospital in Antung

but it was very hard to walk away from the children in the orphanage.

The 125-bed hospital had opened in 1906. It contained two sections; one was called the Men's Hospital and the other, the Women's Hospital. It was staffed by several Danish doctors and nurses throughout the years, and a large number of Chinese doctors and nurses were trained there. Karen Gormsen, a Danish missionary with whom I had become acquainted when I first came to China, was the hospital's first midwife and nurse. She had accomplished great things in this setting. As a midwife she gained access into the homes of local people, and in this way she was able to identify and meet the needs of many women. As time went on her heart went out to all the little girls who were born only to be rejected. Many were sold into brothels, and most were abused. Her tender heart drove her into all types of impossible situations - arguing, bargaining, and sacrificing to save the children and mothers. Hundreds of children came to the orphanage that Karen established. In this institution they were clothed, fed, and trained to become leaders. Out of the medical mission were created many clinics. These became stations to reach out in love to the people around the country. We prayed for the success of this work.

Beginning of the end

When I arrived in Antung, Andrea Nielsen was the supervising nurse of the Women's Hospital. Within a year of my arrival she became ill and was sent to Mukden for her health. I took over her role at the hospital. Around this time we started to see the beginning of the end for our mission work. Paul H. Baagø wrote in his study book for supporters, "It was not the persecution of the missionaries or the opposition to Christianity that was the real reason for the missionaries to leave from China, Japan, Korea, and Manchuria. It was the war preparations and the war." The last two and one half years were truly eventful and unforgettable as supplies ran out and could not be purchased. Patients obtained drugs necessary to their health on the black market. The dire need for medications and supplies caused many thefts, so it was important to keep an eye on all things. Sick and worried people were the only things in plentiful supply.

Dr. Bi's example of faith

In the Women's Hospital I worked with Dr. Bi and Dr. Li. Dr. Bi was the elder of the two and had worked with Danish doctors and nurses for many years. She was also well versed in Chinese customs and had a good knowledge of the people, so she could always be relied upon as an intermediary when needed. Dr. Li was young and quite a recent convert to Christianity. She came from a wealthy Chinese family in Peking where she had also received her medical training. When the Japanese took Peking, she moved to Manchuria to Mukden Medical College, which was a Scotch-Presbyterian

Dr. Li

53

Mission where Dr. Pedersen and his wife spent their last years. When the Japanese invaded Mukden, Dr. Li moved to Antung.

Every morning the staff met for devotions which we took turns leading. We stood in a circle in a large, clean room in the clinic. One particular morning, it was Dr. Bi's turn. Sadly, the night before we had heard that her brother, a teacher, and her younger sister, a doctor, had been taken in the middle of the night and imprisoned. I prepared myself for taking over the devotions. The next morning everyone was on time, and all were sobered by the news of Dr. Bi's family. Dr. Bi entered the room with her Bible. She began to recite Psalm 37 from memory.

Do not fret because of evil men or be envious of those who do wrong; for like the grass they will soon wither, like green plants they will soon die away. Trust in the Lord and do good; dwell in the land and enjoy safe pasture. Delight yourself in the Lord and he will give you the desires of your heart. Commit your way to the Lord; trust in him and he will do this: He will make your righteousness shine like the dawn, the justice of your cause like the noonday sun. (NIV)

On and on Dr. Bi recited, committing her family to the Lord and asking for protection and courage for all of us. When she had finished, we were all encouraged once more. How much we needed that! We continued to pray for Dr. Bi's family for a month. Then miraculously they were released! In many similar situations the Chinese never saw their dear ones again; often the loved ones were tortured and killed.

The door up is always open

The concerns we carried in our hearts were widespread; war covered the globe. In my case 1943 was the year that the Danish police were disarmed by the Nazis and most of the Danish Jews were rescued from the infamous death camps in Germany by being smuggled to Sweden. German cities were bombed by the British. I did not know all the details of my family's life during this time until the war ended and I was back home in Denmark again. Yet I continued to pray for them as they prayed for me, and we trusted that our prayers were heard. Years later reflecting back on that time, I can see even more clearly how well the prayer chain that stretched across continents worked, that is, how God responded to our prayers. As my father wrote in the last letter that would get through to me, "Remember when all other doors are closed, the door up is always open."

The war spirit is everywhere

Meanwhile back in Antung Hospital in China the war spirit was everywhere and affected everything we did. The food was becoming increasingly scarce, and supplies were running out. A very serious effect of the famine was

54

the many cases of difficult childbirth caused by osteomalacia, a deterioration of the bones related to vitamin D deficiency. Women suffered indescribably before they were brought to us. They were often in labor for several days, and if cesarean sections were not performed, the babies would be stillborn.

At times I would receive directives from the Japanese not to go to the hospital until I was notified. When I received the green light to go to the hospital, perhaps around noon, I found the doctors had been required to stay in one room and most of the nurses in another. Two staff members were ordered to go around with the police who went through charts and doctors' orders to make certain we were not concealing people whom they considered enemies.

We carried on with training the nurses as best we could. Thursday evenings we shared Bible study and prayer meeting with the student nurses. Every morning Dr. Li and I would meet in her room for prayer. The missionaries held services in the school for missionary children after we could no longer safely meet in the church. In January, 1945, the Japanese police arrested one of our young Danish pastors. As we gathered for worship on Sunday night, we all prayed for Jacob. The pastor based his sermon that night on Psalm 46, *"The Lord Almighty is with us; the God of Jacob is our fortress."* (Psalm 46:7, NIV).

Jacob's story

Following is Jacob Gejlsbjerg's story in his own words translated from a Danish report in the book, *Sun Rays from a Time of Darkness*, prepared for the Danish Mission Society in 1946.

One Month in a Chinese Prison

It started with one of the usual visits by a Chinese policeman to our mission station in Feng Huang Ch'eng. He asked me to go with him to the police station. It was not the first time he had come nor was it the first time he had asked me to go there with him. I was a little irritated at him for disturbing me as it was time for supper. Gerda Beck had also been summoned and was with me. [Gerda was not imprisoned.] On the way there I began to feel a little uneasy and had a premonition that this was going to be a very uncomfortable experience. Why did he come to get me at this late hour? I felt very anxious when I was brought before the higher authorities, all Japanese officials except for one Chinese man who translated.

After several questions, some very unpleasant and others rather foolish, the chief policeman gave a sign to take me out. I thought I was being taken to another room for further interrogation, and I asked the man who accompanied me where I was going. He refused to answer me. Suddenly he stopped at the end of a hall. On one side there were two small windows that looked out to a high wall; the other side of the hall had four rooms with cross bars facing the hall. I still had no idea what was happening to me, and I did not know where I was. I said, "The stench is terrible here. Is it a pig sty or dunghill in there?" He answered me by commanding me to take off my coat. He also took my watch, glasses, belt, tobacco, and money. Then I knew I was being impris-

oned and asked myself, "Is this happening because of the Gospel or for some other reason?" After taking off my shoes, I was pushed into one of the cells. A lock was put on the door.

This happened on January 5, 1945, just before the celebration of Epiphany. The room I was put into was about 3 by 2.86 meters, and there was absolutely no furniture. A mysterious raw board box with a lid stood in one corner, and 13 Chinese men sat around on the wooden floor eating. There was no window; the only light came through the crossbars and from one electric bulb hanging from the ceiling. There was no stove although it was minus 18 degrees Celsius outside (about minus 4 degrees Fahrenheit). In the hall outside the cell stood a little charcoal stove that was meant to heat all four cells.

The Chinese prisoners did not say anything to me at first but offered to share a little lump of their corn bread. I just had lost my appetite because I realized from where the terrible stench was emanating; the mysterious box in the corner was our toilet. The sight of the Chinese alone was enough to take away my appetite. Sitting for weeks or months like that without a chance to get washed, shaved or have a hair cut, without a change of clothes, never out in the fresh air, just has to make anybody very unappealing to behold. After one month, I did not look any better than the others.

The first couple of hours I was so stunned I could not say anything to the Chinese who began to speak to me. I kept thinking there was some real misunderstanding, that I would be let out after a few hours, but, alas, this was not the case. At 10:00 the watchman bellowed out that we should lie down and go to sleep. There was no bedding. I got my coat and fur cap which I spread out on the floor to sleep on, beside all the other men, but of course, no sleep came. It was too cold. The colonies of vermin coming from the man next to me kept me awake, but from him I also got a little warmth. The cold was worse than the vermin. The next morning three more prisoners were brought in to share our room. Now we could not all sleep at one time. It is impossible to sleep with another man's legs on top of you. We tried but found that it did not work, so we slept only in turns. My legs were the longest of all, so I had more trouble than most.

I spent one month in this hole. We only came out when we were to be interrogated, tortured, or whipped. The first night seemed so unbearable that I didn't think I could survive it. The stench almost choked me. Those who know me would hardly call me sensitive, but this was intolerable, so much so that the guard held his nose when he came by every hour. My old bladder infection made me even more miserable.

When day came the next morning, I felt that I had aged many years. At 10:00 A.M. a little trap door was opened. Cornbread and a piece of turnip were thrown in to us. A little later a bowl of water went the rounds. That was the only water we saw - two times a day. After living like this a month, one resembles a pig more than a human being. I weighed only 100 pounds when I was set free, so in that respect I did not resemble a pig.

When we have nothing to read and nothing to occupy our hands, time gets awfully long. My fellow prisoners were almost all from the lower class of people, those for whom society had no use. They were robbers and opium addicts; they had no spiritual interests. After a few days, thinking I would be here a long time if I lived through it at all, and thinking I would die here, I began to see the opportunity I had to witness. Over

56

half of these men knew nothing of Christianity. I knew I had a wonderful opportunity to share Jesus Christ with them. I also knew the Japanese police had given orders that the guard should report if I said anything. The first couple days I was quiet, but then that was the end of my silence.

One day in prison under these circumstances is very long, and after talking several hours one gets very tired. We were not allowed to lie down during the day, neither were we allowed to get up and stretch our legs. So we just sat there on the bare floor staring at the black walls hour after hour. We tried to warm our hands and feet by sitting on them. Sometimes I would put my bare feet in my fur cap. The soles of our stockings were worn out in a few days. The only exercise occurred when we chased vermin every other hour all night long.

In that month I learned much about God. That type of knowledge is seldom acquired on good days. I learned to pray in a way that is only learned in deepest despair with the thought of death at the doorstep. I did not really see death as a good friend. I was not afraid to die, but very sad to leave this world without being able to say goodbye to my family and friends.

The last four to five days, I was very ill. I could not concentrate and could hardly pray the Lord's Prayer. Then the miracle happened! February 1 at 4:00 P.M. I was sent home because of my illness. The Japanese did not want foreigners to die in their imprisonment, in spite of their daily threats to cut off my head. Then why was I imprisoned? I cannot say much about this painful subject, only this. The Japanese police officer who ordered my imprisonment said in one of the interrogation periods that I had said untimely things about him and Japan and that I had refused to help Japan win this holy war by not allowing the mission property used for military services and as a Danish missionary I had a bad influence on the Chinese because of the mission's stand against national ceremonies [bowing to Shinto]. A few months after the capitulation [of Japan], this Japanese officer was shot by Chinese communists, together with another of my torturers. He was a very wicked man and deserved his fate.

Many have asked me what the worst of this imprisonment was - dirt, filth, vermin? Yes, they were all bad, but from our Maker's hand, man has been given a unique ability to survive, surely the Chinese much more so than Europeans. Unless we have had a poor upbringing, we can get used to unbelievable circumstances when they are forced upon us. The food was bad and insufficient. The first week we were served cornbread and turnip which at this time was as good as the poor Chinese lived off, year after year without complaint. The last three weeks we did not get cornbread, but a millet porridge. It was so poor that even the Chinese had a hard time eating it. Still, the filth, vermin, and poor food were not the worst. Lonesomeness and separation - being totally separated from family - were very hard. These seemed harder on the Chinese than on me. They wanted to know how I could stay so calm. They cried and complained calling on their mothers every night. I knew the answer, but before I had a chance to explain, someone said, "The minister believes in God and we don't, so he never feels all alone."

The worst of all were the interrogation sessions. Three times I was brought out to be questioned in front of an audience of Japanese and a few Chinese. The Chinese were told how they should treat the white man. My interrogator pulled me by the hair *around the room, or he would hit and kick me or demand that I get down on the floor in front of him, knocking my head against the floor as the heathen did in front of their idols. One time he struck me with a hot stoker so that most of my hair was burned. Most of all, he enjoyed scoffing and mocking me and all missionaries. He said that we all wore masks, that we came to the East to exploit the local people, that we acted as if we loved the Chinese, but we were all a band of hypocrites and embezzlers. He vowed he would do what he could to open the eyes of the Chinese. According to him, all Christianity was one great delusion, and Christ was a swindler and his disciples had learned well from Him. Initially I tried to explain, but it was hopeless to discuss with such a man. He hollered, "Shut up, or I will cut off your head!" This type of scorn was hard to hear when the most precious thing upon which our whole lives were built was trampled and I could not say a word. Even now I have sleepless nights - a little less as time goes on.*

In the cell beside me was my good friend and co-worker, Reverend Yao. He came out the day after I did because of his connection with the mission. He had suffered frostbite and was sick for several months after he was released. While in prison we were not allowed to speak with each other, but once in a while we could sneak in a comforting word. We were glad we had each other as fellow sufferers and prayer partners. I often heard him witness to his fellow prisoners about Jesus Christ.

I do not wish another month like it, but God never told me that it was a mistake or, as I had hoped, that He felt sorry for me. He said something entirely different, "Learn to trust in my Grace alone." I learned that. We human beings have no right to claim anything and no right to complain. There is only one thing we can and must do - hope and wait upon God's mercy.

Shortly after his imprisonment Jacob was able to get out of China, and he returned to Denmark.

6

Soviet Occupation & Chinese Civil War

God is our refuge and strength, an ever-present help in trouble. Psalm 46:1 (NIV).

Defeat of the Japanese

After the bomb was dropped on Hiroshima on August 6, 1945, the whole world seemed shaken. The nazis and fascists grew more nervous as did the Chinese. In Antung, where many Japanese officials had been in charge, we saw firsthand what happened to them. Revenge, that had been seething in the hearts of the Chinese people, burst like a tornado, sweeping through the land and leaving destruction everywhere.

There was no organized leadership to take over the rule of the country. During the 14 years that the Japanese had ruled, the Manchurian Chinese had been stripped of people who could lead. All possible candidates had been imprisoned, killed, or coerced into servitude. They had been brainwashed in school from the time they were very young all the way through their youth. To keep alive through the years, some had acted as if they had mental retardation or were insane.

The bomb caught everyone by surprise. During the night the Chinese took all the officials and as many other Japanese as possible. It was told that 800 of them were transported into Siberia! Whatever happened, all we knew is that they disappeared overnight. We were greeted in the morning by the news that a little Japanese mother, whose husband had been taken, had come to the hospital with her five children. She had a gash in her head. It was unheard of that a Japanese individual would seek out a Chinese doctor or hospital!

That morning I needed to go out to pick up my calling cards, which were necessary for travel or doing business. Dr. Li insisted on going with me, not knowing what could happen. I really did not want her to be seen with me for fear she would be mistreated if she was associated with me, but I was very happy to know of her courage and her concern for me. In the city all Japanese businesses were closed; everything was in chaos.

The struggle between the 8th Army (the Communists) and Chiang Kai Shek's forces became evident immediately. The Nationalist Chinese signed a treaty that allowed Russia two months to help keep peace. The irony was very apparent. There would be no peace! The two months became five months. The Russian soldiers who were also very poor and who had been denied many privileges went amok. They felt they had the right to stop people and especially to deprive them of their wristwatches. Some were said to have a whole row of watches on their arms.

Rape by the Russians became all too common. At this point we still could travel somewhat. The elder missionaries were eager to get the children and youth from Danish missionary families and business people out of the country. I was also given the chance to leave. I remember asking myself the question, "How would Dad feel if you flee the sinking ship?" I could not leave the young nurses who needed us more than ever.

Now we did not know who our real friends were. The Communists got the upper hand in South Manchuria. They called us together often to give us lectures on all the benefits they had to offer. Now our dear young people received more brainwashing! Civil war broke out around us. At one time several hundred wounded men were lodged around the hospital, and the Chinese staff was commandeered to care for them.

There was a two-week lull between the fall of the Japanese and the settling in of the Communist forces. During this time we were able to buy some goods from the storehouses of the Japanese. We were thrilled to buy bolts of cotton cloth that our seamstress busily sewed into sheets and pillowcases that we needed so badly. Our joy over these items was short-lived. Clothes dryers were unheard of at this time, and the muggy summer weather made it difficult to dry clothes completely in a day. One night the new bed linens were stolen off the clothesline.

With the Communist take-over the atrocities and pogroms - organized persecution and massacres - started all over again. The Mayor of Antung was paraded around town with a dunce cap on his head and a large sign hung around his neck debasing him. Under the Communists this sort of thing happened to the wealthiest people.

Protection of the student nurses

The testing of our faith took many forms. Rumor came that the army wanted our nurses to follow them and serve in the army. For the women, serving in the army meant providing for the men's "comfort;" in other words, they were likely to be raped. Dr. Li and I, and of course all the others, prayed for God's protection of them. Many of our nursing students were very young and did not even want to go home on their vacations or days off because they felt safer with us. After weeks of uncertainty the order came that the army did indeed want our nurses. The next order was that they wanted 13 nurses. Dr. Li was petite and young-looking; she decided to wear a nurse's uniform and go with the young women so that she could comfort them. I will never forget that night when we gathered in the classroom where Dr. Li and I had the task of choosing the 13 who would go with the army. How could we do that!? We could all pray, and we did. Then I was asked to give a little talk. I clearly recall the gist of it. "In our countries in times of war we must all heed the governments' orders. You also are called to go and you cannot say no. During your time here in the mission hospital, you have experienced how God has protected and kept you. Now put your trust in God. The same God who protected you in the hospital will protect you in the field." We gathered a wash basin for each of the women who would be leaving and filled them with necessary toiletries, which were very scarce, and copies of the Gospel of John. We then had the young women draw lots. Initially those who did not have to go showed their joy. Then suddenly all began to wail and cry for the ones who faced the upcoming ordeal. It was heart-rending, and we suffered with them and prayed.

We were not told when the soldiers would come for the nurses. I told the young women that no matter when they came, night or day, they were to call me; I would come and see them off. Another few weeks passed in which we did not hear from the army. Finally one morning the order came. The 13 met with Dr. Li and me for prayers in Dr. Li's room. The wait seemed interminable. Then at noon we received the message that the trucks had come and a revised order was issued. They now wanted only 11 nurses. Again we drew lots. Again the immediate joy of the two lucky ones quickly dissolved into grief for all the others. Once more we waited. The last message came late in the afternoon. The trucks were gone, and the soldiers had all left! The army had moved on without taking any of our young nurses! Now the grief turned into praise, for we all had experienced God's wonderful power and mercy!

Helping the children survive

The winter of 1945-46 was very cold and extremely difficult. On one occasion the electricity went out. For two weeks we had all we could do to keep the patients warm. The curtains were all taken down and padded to make warmer coverlets for the baby cribs. Dr. Li was a great knitter. She brought me a pair of heavy stockings that she knit from strands of cotton, silk, and wool. We wore padded homemade shoes and cotton padded Chinese outfits. During my free time I crawled into bed to read or rest. Only God knows how we all made it through.

The days ahead were not very encouraging. This would be the last winter

Nurses and student nurses caring for babies in the cold winter in China.
The blankets in the cribs were made from curtains.

in China for my colleagues and me. It proved to be a testing time for all of us.
Coal for the stoves in the orphanage was very scarce, and finally only coal dust
was available. Karen Gormsen suffered terribly to see the lack of food for her
dear orphan children, and of course, the home was filled with many needy
children. Through so many years Karen had helped people all around; when
they could, those people reciprocated her kindnesses. One fall day some Chinese friends brought three pheasants to the orphanage. They had used stones
to kill the birds since they did not have guns. On another occasion I found
Karen standing on the back porch with a basketful of old apples, which were
bruised and quite spoiled. Yet, all the children took one as they filed by, and
all said, "Thank you."

One day a baby was found in the trash can in the hospital. Where could the
baby go? The reply, as usual, was that Karen would care for the child. Another day when I was walking home from the hospital, there was a little bundle
outside the gate to the orphanage. That was not unusual. Sometimes the moth-

62

ers would peek around a corner to make certain their precious babies were picked up. I tried to help out in the orphanage. I would go there at mealtime, when I left the hospital for the night, and during my time off. Karen herself took care of the very sick babies. Often I would find her sitting by the side of a crib holding a tiny baby's hand.

Over the years many of the children were educated and in time became leaders, educators, and parents. Karen, who never married, became a loving "grandmother" to many!

Confrontations

I had a routine of going to the hospital every night at 10:00 o'clock to see if all was well and to say good night to the student nurses and staff. It was difficult to do this because the Communists enforced a complete blackout. All windows had to be covered so that no light shone out into the street. I had to walk about a block through an alley which was very dark. The sentries who guarded our gate were often very young and had been given the authority to shoot anybody whom they thought looked suspicious. As a rule the same sentry guarded the gate to the orphanage and the one to the hospital. When I would leave for the hospital, I would tell the guard who I was and what I was planning to do. On two occasions the guards changed. One night when I tried to enter the hospital gate, which was really a locked door, I was confronted with a gun and kept there until I could convince the man who I was. On another night, even though I did not stay long at the hospital, I was stopped as I came back to the orphanage. The guard was very jittery. He cocked his rifle and held me at bay. Yet, I felt at perfect peace. Somehow I knew that he could not pull that trigger.

Formidable sentry

Every missionary in China had her or his own story to tell. It was not until I was in Africa several years later that I learned of Olga Kristensen's last days in China. Olga had moved to Chin Chou in 1919, where a large congregation quickly grew from her faithful work. Toward the end of World War II, the Russian Communist soldiers were plundering and raping. Their usual mode of attack was to seize one street at a time, looting, raping, and leaving all in chaos. They seemed to have been especially barbarous in Chin Chou. Nearly thirty women had been raped before they took their families and sought refuge in the mission station. Olga ushered them all into the church, which was the only place large enough to accommodate them. One evening her ears caught the noise and tumult of the troops, and she knew they would be the next victims. She was very concerned about the panic-stricken women and withdrew to her room to pray. Out of the blue she heard a voice read the words of Proverbs 3:24-26.

Dr. Li and Dagamar with two sick children

When you lie down, you will not be afraid; when you lie down, your sleep will be sweet. Have no fear of sudden disaster or of the ruin that overtakes the wicked, for the Lord will be your confidence and will keep your foot from being snared. (NIV)

Olga could not remember where these verses were written so she asked God to show her. The answer came to her, and she rushed over to the church and read the scripture verses for the women. They all got down on their knees and thanked God because He had already set them free. Outside the walls the tumult continued, but the women laid down and went to sleep in peace. Olga decided to lie down with her clothes on so that she would be ready if anything happened during the night. God spoke to her again and rebuked her lack of faith. Then Olga undressed, went to bed, and slept through the night.

Next morning the town was a mess. The neighbors' homes were in complete disarray. Outside the gate there were three dead bodies. No one had even knocked on the door to the mission station. Later three Chinese Communists - called "small legs" because they assisted the Russians - knocked on the door and asked to see Olga. Tearfully, they asked her what sort of countrymen she had hired as sentries for the mission. She asked them to explain what the sentries looked like. They told her the sentries were shining figures standing around the wall. Outside the gate a figure of light stood with a crown of jewels and a large sword. When the figure moved, lightening ran from it out into the street. These figures scared the soldiers so much that they did not dare attack the mission. Olga never saw the radiant figures, but she told the trembling Communists, "You be careful not to get in their way. They will destroy you."

64

7

Leaving China:
He led us all the way

See, I am sending an angel ahead of you to guard you along the way and to bring you to the place I have prepared. Exodus 23:20 (NIV).

Our faith journey begins

Over the years in China, in spite of all the adversity and opposition, God planted seeds of Christianity through the missionaries. These seeds seemed to sprout and grow. Given the political climate in 1946, we knew that we could not continue our work there. It was time to leave our dear Christian friends in the care of God and return home to Denmark.

It was early morning, June 19, 1946, when we assembled at the station in Antung (later called Dandong), Manchuria, to start on our faith journey home to Denmark. I called it our faith journey because of the destruction, devastation, and deceit all around us and our lack of protection and resources for the trip. Only by faith could we believe that we would make it safely back home again. There were 14 of us Danish missionaries - seven single women who were teachers and nurses, and one family, the Rev. Kaj Olsen, his wife Johanne, who was a nurse, and their five children, three girls and two boys, ages eight to sixteen. The youngest boy contracted polio as a baby and walked with a limp.

The day was gray and damp. It was as if that spring morning had caught the mood of uncertainty of the times and the people. Some of us had been in China nine years and some fourteen without going back to Denmark for a furlough. Our hope of seeing family and dear friends once again mingled with our sorrow at leaving our Chinese friends who had become like family to us under the Japanese occupation. Our mixed emotions along with the downfall of the Japanese, the Russian invasion of China, the bitter civil war between the

The Kaj Olsen family who walked out of China with Dagmar

nationalists and communist Chinese, and the recent take-over by the communist armies all set the mood for our trip.

Several of the hospital staff had come to say good-bye. They were the most courageous of our friends. Many dared not venture out to see us off for fear of their safety. In those days first term missionaries stayed seven years before returning home. By the time we left, we were all past due for a furlough, but how we dreaded leaving the young nursing students who relied so much on us for security! With our departure the mission would be left entirely in the hands of the inexperienced Chinese staff. The Chinese communists, who were unfriendly towards western and religious influences, were winning the war. The mission might not survive. Our decision to leave was made when we realized that our staying would make life more difficult for the hospital staff because our Chinese friends could be questioned by authorities or even killed for associating with us. We also could not work effectively under existing conditions. The hospital was depleted of medicine and all supplies necessary for medical treatments.

We essentially had our bags packed for about three years while we watched and waited for the safest time to leave. Our opportunity came when a two-week cease-fire was declared, and after two Danish boys who had left Manchuria earlier sent word from Peking that they were safe. The two 18-year-olds had been stranded in Manchuria with their families. One was the son of a missionary; the other was the son of a businessman who worked for a Danish shipping company in Japan. Both had attended the mission school for Danish

66

children in Antung. One day the two young men disappeared. Their parents searched for them and finally located them in jail. The two had been arrested by the Russians after they had gone to the Russian authorities to determine the possibility of leaving the area. They were held for a day and a night. After their release they disappeared again. This time their parents had a good idea what they were doing. Without telling their families, they left to find a way out of China. Previously we had all been told that this was impossible.

After the Japanese surrender following the bombing of Hiroshima, the Chinese people expressed their frustration and hatred through vandalism and destruction of all that reminded them of that era. Manchuria had been the Japanese paradise, rich in minerals, silks, fruit, rice, and other grains. The Japanese had built the South Manchurian Railway that connected with the Trans-Siberian Railway. It went all the way through Manchuria and gave good access to Peking. A portion of the railway was built through the mountainous area and had many tunnels. The entire Japanese administrative network, where top officials had been stationed, was located in this area. (Japan had sent only the best to overlook their paradise.) This part of the country, therefore, was extremely dangerous because of current vandalism and destruction by the Chinese. The two young men, however, found a way safely through to Peking, even though it had been a long trek by foot. They sent word to their parents, who also were able to negotiate their way to Peking. Now, with the cease-fire, the governing body of the mission determined that it was our chance to attempt escape. Thus began our perilous journey back to Denmark.

We started out that dreary June morning not knowing what we would encounter. We had a long journey ahead of us; much of it would be on foot. We would be traveling first northwest to Mukden (now Shenyang), next southwest to Peking (now Beijing), and then southeast to Shanghai. We entrained in Antung. The train had been vandalized: glass was missing from the windows and there were no seats or lights, but we could sit on our suitcases and other bundles, and we were headed home! The scenery was gorgeous that spring day. Wherever God's handiwork was still intact, we feasted on its beauty instead of staring at the vandalism.

Blessings and challenges along the way

Late in the afternoon we reached Tsao-He-Kou, which was halfway between Antung and Mukden. The train did not go further. The Olsens stayed with a Christian family whom they knew. We women stayed at the inn and slept on the *kang*. The family with whom the Olsens stayed invited friends and additional family members to visit in the evening. They asked Pastor Olsen to speak to them and conduct a communion service. Back at the inn where we women stayed, the owner also asked us to have a meeting, so, we closed another chapter of our service worshiping with our hosts.

On the second day of our trip we walked 60 li, about 20 miles, from Tsoa-He-Kuo to Hsia-Ma-Tang. The Olsen children did very well. They had grown up in China and were accustomed to walking everywhere. The youngest son who had a limp walked partway, was carried by family members at times, and rode a donkey when one was available. Our group had now expanded to include 14 Chinese men who helped us carry our baggage. We stopped for a little rest at a small inn and improvised a meal. We rested until about four o'clock in the afternoon. In this area we could walk on the tracks because no trains were running. This railroad system, that had been the pride of the Japanese, was finished just the previous year. Now devoid of trains that would have been carrying well-to-do passengers of many nationalities, it came in handy for us as we tried to walk the shortest distance possible to our destination.

We were headed north, and we had to pass through one of the long railroad tunnels that had been carved through the mountains. It was completely dark in the tunnel, and we held hands to be sure that we were all together. In the tunnel we ran into Koreans and others who were headed south, trying to escape China and return to their homeland. It was raining when we exited at the other end. In fact, it poured, and we were soaked to the skin. Even our little money bags, which we had sewn into our clothes, were wet. What a day! We were sunburned, hot, tired, and now drenched!

Fortunately we found a large inn that could take all of us. It was a night to be remembered. We changed clothes and hung them as best we could from the ceiling. While our Chinese baggage carriers slept across the other side of the room, all 14 of us Danes were lined up on the *kang*, the Olsen family on one end and the seven women on the other. With our wet clothes dripping down on us, and our swollen feet and legs up against the wall, we were packed on the *kang* so tightly that we all had to turn over at the same time. But we were together, and we were on our way home; that was all that mattered at the time.

As would happen many times, the communists came before we left to inspect our luggage and see our permits. We never knew for certain what they thought they might find - weapons, perhaps, or something that looked subversive. They even examined our shoes. While this was an unnerving experience, it became commonplace. We trusted in God to keep us from harm and prayed that He would surround us with angels for protection.

A premature end to the cease-fire.

At 5:30 A.M. the next morning, we started up the mountain pass on our way to Kung Yuan over the Han-Ling Pass. As we finally reached the top of the hill, we were stopped by a couple of sentries. They refused to let us go on. It was impossible to negotiate with them. Reluctantly we turned around and made our way down the hill that we had just conquered, but before heading down, we sat for a few minutes viewing the beautiful scenery. From where we sat we could see two of the railroad tunnels below.

At the foot of the mountain we stopped to determine our next move. We got some boiling water from one of the nearby families. Not knowing what to do next, we sat down by the river in the shade of some trees while the Rev. Olsen went to the village to seek out some of the authorities who perhaps could give us some sort of permission or information that would help us decide what to do. Mrs. Olsen went to a nearby home to get her shoe repaired. The sole had come apart and finally had fallen off. The rest of us ate some hard boiled eggs which had been given to us by a Chinese Christian. This was a generous gift. Eggs were very expensive then at $3.50 a piece! While we waited, we enjoyed the mountains and the lush grass, which felt so cool and refreshing that hot morning.

We had devotions in that beautiful locale and sang some of our meaningful Danish hymns, such as "Commit Your Way to God." While we sang the hymn, "Mysterious are the Ways of the Lord," an explosion filled the air and shook the ground around us. A second one followed. As we looked around, we realized that both of the tunnels had been blown up. Within a few seconds' time, the huge engineering wonder was forever gone. Chunks of fiery stone and rubble fell in the river by our side. The temporary truce had been broken early. Miraculously we all escaped injury.

The Rev. Olsen hurried back, relieved to see that we were all right. He had watched the destruction from the office window of the Chinese Communists. Permission to travel forward had been given very reluctantly. "Go back to Antung; you will never make it," he was initially told. Officials told him that it was impossible to continue north which was the shortest route. There was one way left, through a valley, but the valley was known for the hoards of bandits ravaging people there. Officials reported, "They will, as a rule, not kill but will take all you have." We listened to Pastor Olsen's report, then discussed our options. We all said that we wanted to continue home, for we felt certain that we should go on, since God had led us safely this far. One of the baggage carriers said to us, "We will go with you because your God is with you."

Changing direction meant that we had to cross a river that we had struggled to cross that very morning. The river was wide but only a meter deep. The only bridge was a very narrow boardwalk which would swing and teeter with each step we took as we followed each other across. Some of the group plunged in, feeling it was better to wade across rather than topple in unexpectedly. One of the carriers did fall in with the luggage for which he was responsible.

It was about 10:00 A.M. when we started again. Behind us, up on the mountain pass, the war had started again. Not far out of town we stopped once more. Fearing for their lives, some of the baggage carriers went on strike and refused to go any farther with us. After hiring new carriers, we started again on our journey of faith.

From no-man's-land to nationalist territory

After three hours of walking, we stopped at a large farm where we were all given warm meals. We rested two hours and then went on our way again. The scenery in this valley was a joy to behold. It surpassed in beauty anything we had seen. All the way up the mountain pass and down again, the valley was lush with rich growths of flowers and trees punctuated by mountain springs and rippling brooks. The air was pure and clean! There was a holy quietness to this place that was soothing to our weary bodies. Although we did see some suspicious groups on the mountain sides, we were not approached by any of them. No shots were heard, no masses of people were present, and we saw no destruction resulting from human hands. We were away from the eyes of our gestapo, the Japanese who watched and questioned everything we did, and from the lectures of the new captors, the Chinese Communists. In spite of our physical weariness, all of us seemed invigorated.

On the fourth day of our journey, June 22, we were ready to start anew after enjoying a good breakfast of chicken and *kao-liang* porridge. *Kao-liang* was a type of sorghum grain which was very common and grew well in China. It was eaten when rice was scarce. By 6:00 A.M. we were on our way once more, but already by 7:00 A.M. we were stopped by guards. We had just travelled through no-man's-land and were about to enter into the Nationalists' territory. Here we were told that we could not be seen walking out of town. We must hire some wagons, which would be driven by Chinese Communists. In this way they could maintain control by keeping an eye on us and preventing us from roaming. After some searching and dickering, we were relieved to get a ride, but we were also relieved of 7000 yen for the use of three to four wagons. It was 50 li (about 17 miles) to the station where we hoped to entrain.

The 17-mile ride took all day. We arrived at Han Ling, which was at the border of the territory held by the Nationalists, around 5:00 P.M. This time we were stopped by two soldiers. They were concerned about the Chinese men, including the guide who accompanied us. These were the usual suspicions that accompanied movement from territory occupied by one group into the territory of the other group. We were greeted by a Chinese advisor to the police or the army; fortunately he was very polite. We found a little business where we could get some food, and we ate a real treat of *mien chiaotze* (a noodle-like delicacy made of wheat flour). We were told that we could sleep there for the night. There was room on the *kang* for eight of us; the rest of us would sleep on the floor. The chickens that usually wandered around the *kang* were caged for the night. We then received very good news! The police told us that we could catch a train the following morning that would take us all the way to Mukden.

The night was uncomfortable for those of us who slept on the floor. The floor was uneven, and the boards would move up and down as we turned. The air was stifling down there between the *kangs*; however, we made it through the night with our good humor intact!

We left Han Ling at 8:30 A.M. on June 23 without any inspection of the baggage that we had been told would happen That was quite a relief! The trip to Liao Yang was quite memorable. We rode in a cattle car and sat on our suitcases. On that short trip we saw the ruins of five bridges, a factory, and many other buildings - the cruel aftermath of the war.

70

In Liao Yang the platform was full of people waiting and hoping for a chance to get on the train. The train had no schedule, and we waited for two hours before the black monster come chugging into the station. The whining, shrill whistle filled the clear bright day. To us it sounded as if it was saying, "Maybe, maybe, maybe, maybe," until it screeched to a stop. The train was already filled when it arrived. The most aggressive people got on anyway. The fourteen of us wanted to stay together with our few, very necessary belongings. It did not look good. As always, we turned to God for help and guidance. As we huddled together in the midst of the surging crowd that pushed and shoved like an ocean in a storm, a Chinese gentleman came up to the Rev. Olsen and asked him if we were missionaries. Hearing our reply, he said, "I am a Christian, and I work at this station. I will help you get in." With this, he disappeared into the train, pushing his way through a whole line of cars. Finally he came out the door in one of the rear freight cars. Pushing the people in the car tighter and tighter, he stretched out his hand and one by one pulled all of us into the car. How we all fit, we never will understand. There were no seats, and not much room to stand, but we were on our way in the right direction.

Rest and refreshment at Mukden

At 4:00 P.M. we reached Mukden, our first major destination on our trip homeward. Mr. Tu, a male nurse who had been one of our supervisors in the mission hospital earlier, knew we were coming and was there to meet us. He arranged for wagons to take us across town to the Blind Girls' Home. Seventy girls lived in this home. The supervisor of the home was Miss Li, a dear Chinese Christian friend of ours. The staff and residents of the home had saved rations of rice and coffee for a long time so that they could share them with us if and when we arrived. I had visited the home several times before, and the girls knew me. Miss Li asked me to visit them to provide encouragement. The girls had experienced many anxious moments during the war and had been through many adversities when their beloved leaders were taken from them.

Miss Li wanted me to have her own room. How good it was to fall into a real bed with clean sheets! The events of the past week, however, took their toll. I was very sick and nauseated for the first night and day at the home. Miss Li took care of me like a mother.

During this time several delegations had come to China to see how they could help. One of these was a group from the United Nations Relief and Rehabilitation Administration (UNRRA). UNRRA was founded in 1943 to give aid to countries liberated from Germany, Japan, Italy and other Axis countries. Emergency aid consisted of food, medicine, and restoration of public services, agriculture, and industry. China was one of the chief beneficiaries of assistance from this organization until 1949 when the organization dissolved and its tasks were transferred to other United Nations' agencies. The UNRRA delegation happened to be staying in Mukden while we were passing through. The Rev. Olsen sought them out to learn about possibilities for transportation

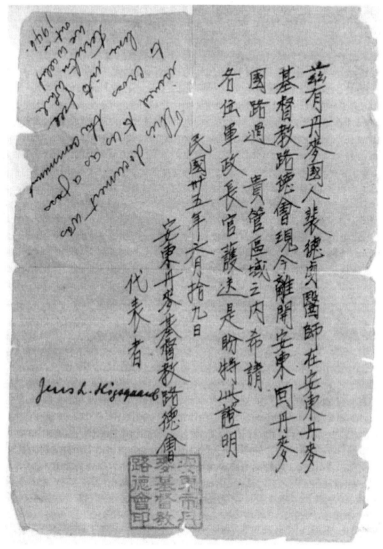

This docutment is to certify that the Danish Dr. Fei De Zhen from the
Danish Christian Lutheran Church at Andong is currently leaving to
return to Denmark and must therefore pass through the territory under
your administration. It is respectfully hoped that the political officials and
military officers in charge will find means of providing an escort.
    June 19th, 1946
    (Signed by) A representatvie of the Danish Christian
Lutheran Church at Andong

The imprint is the official seal of "The Danish Christian Church in
Andong city" and is more unique than a signature.

on the next lap of our journey to Peking. One man from the group brought us a box of cold drinks and other goodies. He asked me where I was from. During our chat, I told him that I had an uncle in Wisconsin. It turned out that he and my uncle were almost neighbors. A few years later, we met again in Wisconsin.

The week at the Blind Girls' Home passed by faster than any other week during these last three years. There was so much for all of us to talk about since there had been no communication during the past three years. There were many friends to see and new friends to make, in addition to helping out in the home.

It was especially encouraging to talk with the doctors and nurses from Mukden Medical Hospital, which was a Christian training center where many of the fine doctors had received their education and where all of us had come to visit Dr. and Mrs. Pedersen and had been inspired by their hospitality. Dr. Pedersen was a Danish doctor who had studied in Scotland, where he met his wife. Weekly their home was filled with young students who came to learn and share. The Pedersens would later go through a time of severe trials and persecutions, but now they told of their daily prayer groups and God's protection and care.

An amazing feast in desolate surroundings

After a week in Mukden, we left for Peking with renewed hope but with great uncertainty regarding whether or not we would ever be able to return to the work and the people whom we loved. We could not help but wonder what our Chinese friends would have to go through in the years to come. We were saddened, yet we continued to anticipate the imminent reunion with families and friends at the end of our long journey.

On the train to Peking we were able to get seats for all of us, even though we were crowded and uncomfortable. We could not see much out of the windows because of the overcrowded conditions. We were the only group of foreigners in a train full of Chinese people, who carried bundles of all shapes and sizes. We had a whole day's journey ahead of us and would reach Peking by night, or so we thought.

The train stopped at several stations. At one of them we heard voices that sounded somewhat familiar. Pastor Olsen pushed his way to the window. Two American men stood outside on the platform. "We heard that there were missionaries on this train, and we brought you a couple of CARE (Cooperative for American Relief to Everywhere) packages," one of them said. The train was off again. Pastor Olsen said to us, "We are going to keep these for later." We always seemed hungry and ready to eat, but how wise was his counsel! As the afternoon faded away, the train stopped somewhere in the open countryside. We did not have to speculate too long on why the train stopped in this location because all of the passengers were soon commandeered off the train with no explanation.

There were no restaurants, hotels or other facilities in sight. We were all thankful for our leader, the Rev. Olsen, who once again contacted the local authorities. We found a large empty building that had been a Japanese office. The windows had all been broken, and all the furniture and fixtures had been removed; yet, this would be our shelter for the night. Without the help of a porter, we wrestled our luggage and the large CARE package filled with goodies to the building. Once there, we separated into two groups - the Olsen family on one end, and the single women on the other. Then we opened the cans and packages in the box of goodies and carefully divided the contents into equal portions. We even found chocolates for dessert! Our mood during the entire trip was one of hope and anticipation, and this particular night we engaged in a great deal of joking, singing, and thanksgiving to God for all His wonderful care. How often since then have we wished that we could thank the two men who provided us not only nourishment but also a good dose of encouragement by this amazing feast during an unanticipated layover. We spent the evening on the cement floor without much bedding, but it seemed adequate for that night.

Recuperation in Peking

The next morning we were all set to go once again. We packed up our belongings and then waited until a train came. We were fortunate that the Japanese train system was still intact in this area; however, there were no schedules. Luckily, one came that day. The train was filled with military personnel, but we were allowed on board. After a day of travel, we arrived in Peking.

Although Peking had changed much from the time we had studied the Chinese language there, it still had the familiar sights and sounds. We stayed at the College of Chinese Studies, the American-built institution where we had studied the Chinese language years before. No studies were taking place, but the staff had prepared lodging for transient missionaries and business people, who for some reason or other still remained in the country. People of all nationalities were looking for passage home. Such transportation was a scarce commodity, so the waiting list was long; our wait was six weeks. The time went fairly fast as we could now take care of many things that had been on the back burner for years, such as visits to dentists and eye doctors.

The hospital in Peking was still somewhat equipped to take care of the most needy. A Danish scientist, Dr. Witt, who had been teaching at a college in Manchuria, developed cancer and was hospitalized in Peking. Several of us nurses took turns providing care for him at night. In spite of his serious condition, he remained cheerful and clear-headed. He made it to Denmark where he died shortly after arrival.

We started recuperating a bit in Peking. Political unrest became more intense during the time we were there, so we were not free to do everything that we wanted to do. However, we ate better, had fellowship with other missionaries, and did a bit of sight-seeing.

74

Denmark via the United States

During this time we learned that Scandinavia was sending two planes, named *St. Paul* and *St. Peter*, to Shanghai to bring home stranded Scandinavian missionaries. This presented us with another challenge - to get to Shanghai. All 14 of us who had walked through Manchuria together were able to obtain passage on an American army plane. This plane was far from being comfortable, but it got us to our destination. Our very first task in Shanghai was to go to the authorities who questioned and searched us. They quizzed me about my Danish passport because they could see by it that I was born in America.

Before we had left for Shanghai, while we were still negotiating for passage home, a request came to the ruling body of our mission group on behalf of three young American women. Three 18-year-olds had become separated from their families and were stranded in China; they were understandably distraught and wanted to return to America as soon as possible. All of the seats on *St. Paul* and *St. Peter* had already been assigned. Our ruling body addressed our group of missionaries and asked if three people would be willing to give up their seats to the young women. Two teachers from our group of 14, Tine Nielsen and Esther Svendsen, readily did so. I gave the request serious thought. I was so concerned about seeing my parents again. Every day that passed seemed another day that I might lose them. I thought how I would never forgive myself if they should die during a delay in my return to Denmark. On the other hand, an alternate passage from China was via ship to America. I was homesick for America and had not been there for 24 years, since I had left with my family for Denmark at the age of 15. I also spoke English fluently and had family and friends in the U.S. I thought if anybody needed to wait and travel through the U.S., it should be I, who had all these resources. So, I made the difficult decision to give up my seat too.

In Shanghai we boarded in a place called "Home Away From Home," which earlier had been a social center for American soldiers. We were offered cots in one of two large rooms. A total of 34 people were staying there at the time waiting for passage home. There was one small bathroom available for all of us to share. It was August and very hot; at times the thermometer hit 104 degrees. Although we felt uncomfortable, we considered ourselves fortunate that we were there in summer rather than enduring the extreme cold of winter.

The questions uppermost in our minds, of course, were who would take us home and when could we go. After spending three weeks in Shanghai, we were able to obtain passage on the next available mode of transportation which was the *U.S.S. General Meiggs*, an American transport liner that had been sent to take stranded refugees home. It could accommodate several thousand people. This was the second such mission after the war had ended. The ship was very crowded with two hundred thirty-four people bunking in one room! These were double bunks, four deep. I was offered one of the lowest bunks. With three people directly above me, I sometimes felt that I would be crushed if the ones above me came crashing down. Again, like Shanghai, it was very hot.

My two friends and I were awestruck by the food on the ship. Passengers were served in cafeteria-style food lines from gleaming stainless steel servers. We had not experienced anything like this before, and the three of us had not seen so much food in ages! It tasted very good, but we found it difficult to enjoy. First, none of us could eat much without becoming sick because we had eaten so little for so long. We also were upset to tears that so much food was thrown away. We had witnessed so much starvation in the past few years. How desperately the starving Chinese people needed this food!

I was seasick the first few days of the trip, not because of storms, but rather the food, heat, emotion, and weariness all seemed to add up and contribute to my discomfort. I happened to be reading the Book of Job at the time. I read that Job was healed after praying for his friends. I thought, "Well, that's one thing I can do while I lie here. I can pray for my friends." After a few days I felt better, and I enjoyed the remainder of the trip over the Pacific. The trip was relaxing and inspirational. Every day brought us one day closer to the hope and excitement of seeing land again. Since I had been homesick for America for so long, I counted the days and hours before I would be there again.

Memorable fellow passengers

I especially enjoyed the fellowship with other passengers. I became acquainted with many of them. There were several groups of people who remain in my heart. The first was a group of young Chinese girls who were on their way to the U.S. Somehow, they had gotten out of China and had been granted passage as refugees. America opened her arms wide to these girls, and the girls were looking ahead excitedly to school in the U.S. I wondered how these girls would adjust to America. Most, if not all, of them had been brought up in mission schools where there were strict moral codes and where the Christian message was an important part of their lives. I had been learning that American schools had been changing since the war. I could not help but be concerned for them.

Another group that interested me was a large group of Catholic nuns. Using their luggage and boxes, they created a private sanctuary for themselves in the midst of the huge dormitory-like room. They woke up early every morning and got together for their devotions. They mostly kept to themselves, yet their very presence and the examples they set were a blessing to us. We knew that the Catholics had been persecuted. We could imagine that they had gone through all kinds of difficulties, and we admired their work, their tenacity, and how they kept their spirits up by singing and praising the Lord.

I met the third memorable group the night we sailed into San Francisco. After days of building excitement, we were told that we would be sailing under the Golden Gate Bridge that very night, September 14, 1946. The night was clear and balmy. I went up on deck quite early. One of the other women came up and said, "Come down and let us know when the bridge is in sight." But I was not going to move from the deck until we had sailed under the bridge.

There was no way I was going to miss a second of that precious view. It meant so much to me. As we were getting closer to San Francisco, I noticed that more and more people were gathering up front. Many of them were Jewish refugees. At least 70 Rabbis had been given permission to study in the U.S. It seemed that the people who were most excited about landing in America were this group of Jewish refugees and me.

Hallelujas under the Golden Gate Bridge

We sailed into San Francisco about 11:00 that night. The bridge was a sight to behold. Of course, it was not only the beauty of the bridge that we beheld, but it was the meaning that we attached to that sight that made it remarkable. For me, nine years in China with all its wonder and its horror were behind me. I was back in the land of my birth. Ahead of me lay reunions with childhood friends, congregations that my father had served during his ministry in the U.S., family members in America, and the ultimate reunion with my family in Denmark. As we came under the bridge the Jewish entourage let out whoops of joy and hallelujas that rang in the skies. I will never forget their joyous shouts. I stood there with tears in my eyes. I was so happy for them. Many of them had travelled for years to become free. They had travelled from Russia, to Siberia, and then China. Now they had made it, and so had I!

8

Around the world
in forty years

Do not store up for yourselves treasures on earth, where moth and rust destroy, and where thieves break in and steal. But store up for yourselves treasures in heaven, where moth and rust do not destroy, and where thieves do not break in and steal. For where your treasure is, there your heart will be also. Matthew 6: 19-21 (NIV).

My reintroduction to America - theft

We had to stand in line a whole day before we could leave the ship. There were all sorts of formalities to attend to, such as going through customs. We were worn out by the time we were able to disembark. When I returned to my bunk to pack my things, I discovered that my best possessions had been stolen while we had been waiting in line. Among the items taken were a small pillow that I had carried around the world with me all these years and a black silk kimono with red lining and red embroidery that I had purchased on sale in Peking years before. This reintroduction to America shook me up. I reminded myself that material possessions were not important. Over the years I had either given up or lost many things. When these items were stolen now, however, when I had so little, it seemed unfair.

America embraces us

As I contemplate this lap of my journey home to Denmark from China in 1946, I realize it is also the last part of my trip around the world in 40 years, due to the fact that I had been born and raised in the U.S.! This lap was important for that reason, but also this six-week period encompassed events that proved to be pivotal in my life - beyond what I ever dreamed. I marvel at how God strategized for me, not only to speak of the mission work and China's plight, but also for me to meet people and experience the thrill of "running into" friends from my parents' previous congregations. It was incredible how visits with others fell into place as I crossed the country. Completely hidden from me at the time was that I was about to meet my future family. .

Although America had recently lost its husbands, fathers, and sons, the war had not touched its soil - except for Pearl Harbor. The stark contrast to China, whose people had suffered the consequences of the drawn-out struggle first against the Japanese, followed by the civil war which ended in communist take-over, put the U.S. in a very rosy image in my eyes. People everywhere accepted us with open arms, eager to make us feel comfortable, to share their love and their homes, to learn of the conditions in China, and to give us gifts for the work of the mission.

After spending a few days in San Francisco and Oakland becoming acquainted with a group of young missionaries waiting there for permission to go into China, Tine Nielsen, Esther Svendsen, and I left for Los Angeles, traveling by train along the Pacific Coast. What a thrill that was compared to the traveling accommodations to which we were accustomed. We felt like queens!

Prior to arriving in Los Angeles, we had obtained the address of A. Kirstine Nielsen, Dr. Niels Nielsen's widow, and arranged to spend time with her. Dr. Nielsen and his wife had been missionaries in China for many years and were still in Suiyen when I spent my first year in Manchuria studying the Chinese language. After I left Suiyen, he had been kidnapped by bandits who expected a large ransom. The bandits had come to the gate of the mission compound calling for the doctor to come to some emergency. For six months he had been dragged around in the surrounding mountains. After he was released, he returned home to L.A.

We were so happy to be together in Mrs. Nielsen's lovely home and had much catching up to do. Boarding in her home was a young chiropractor who persuaded me to receive my first chiropractic treatment. I felt a bit foolish. I, a nurse, getting a chiropractic treatment! I did find that the treatment helped quite a bit. When I became better acquainted with the chiropractor, I learned that he was the son of one of my father's pastoral colleagues.

Esther, Tine, and I parted ways in Los Angeles. This was not a teary farewell, since Denmark is a small country, and missionaries meet often. We knew that we would be spending time together again in the future. Esther and Tine continued east, as they had no relatives or friends in the U.S. This had been their first trip to the U.S.

A missionary should not look like that

Next, I found my Aunt Marie, my father's youngest sister. She was married and had four children. Uncle Otto Christiansen was a contractor and built houses. Their home was in Pacific Palisades. I stayed with them for a week or so. Aunt Marie's first priority was to take me shopping for clothes. I had been carrying a small suitcase which held very few clothes, and I had just received my back pay of $800. I felt wealthy, but actually had no idea what a dollar was worth. The Chinese yen fluctuated as did the Danish krone, and I found inflation just plain confusing. Also, I had handled very little money during the past nine years. Banking business had always been done by our mission treasurer.

Aunt Marie took me to the better stores in L.A. She wanted me to have the best. Being very naive regarding that subject, I followed her initiative and bought high quality clothing - a white wool coat with a matching hat and three gabardine dresses, one for me and one for each of my two oldest sisters, who wore the same size as I. Fifty years later I still have a little coin pouch that was in a $40 purse which I carried for many years.

I had not anticipated what others would think of my new clothes. Someone told me, "A missionary should not look like that." Of course, I understood that later on, realizing that people who gave money for missions never really considered the personal needs of missionaries, only the needs of the people who were served. Mother had always kept us children well-dressed and in style, since she was a professional seamstress. I felt best dressed that way, and I know she at least was glad to see me looking nice when I arrived in Denmark.

Culture shock

Attending church with my aunt, I was mesmerized by the beauty and the well-dressed people. I remember the question that came to mind, "Are these people Christians?" How different they looked from the people whom I had lived and worked with in China! In the afternoon one of my cousins and her family took me to see my first Ice Capades. Again I felt ill at ease - because we were enjoying a performance on a Sunday and because I could not shake the feeling that the money we spent should have gone to relieve the suffering world. I was experiencing culture shock! Riding in a car on the California freeway at night was a shock also. There were so many lights! In China we had lived in a blackout situation for the past several years. My eyes were not accustomed to such brightness at night.

A reunion with Sally and George

Sometime during my stay in L.A., I met Mary Lundsberg. She knew of me, but I had never met her. She was a friend of Sally, my good friend from our church in McNabb, Illinois. Mary had arranged a surprise party for Sally and me to meet. And what a surprise that was! I had not heard from Sally for the past nine years and did not know that she was in California. Sally's brother, George, was my old boyfriend. Sally owned a beauty shop in Burbank. She gave me a permanent and arranged for us to travel together to Phoenix, Arizona, to visit George, who lived there with his wife and children. George and

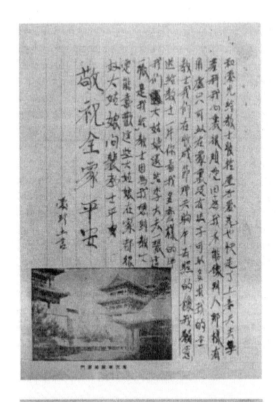

和蒙先的教士說起這才蒙先生忙校走了上李夫夫學
着拜我们喜歡用您
用意只可以如在家裏是有此子可如家裏是我的孝
教士我们在此成…午去聽的候我嚴慈
送給教士一并你看看是嚴慈的
我们
送給教士因為我想到教士
嚴是我好姑娘送交姑娘到我嚴慈
逆能喜歡這些交姑娘在家都很
叔女姑娘向蒙家士平安

敬祝全家平安

榮邦上言

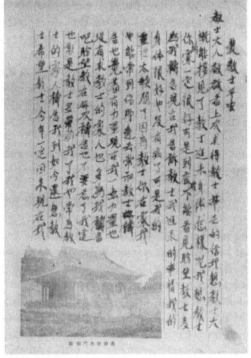

敬教士平安
教士大人敬啟者上次未得教士拜之的信我想起教士大
職能擺見了教士過未到在您這兒我想教士
你家一定很好可是到處不能香見教士我教士愛
然我閣念教士并告訴教士我過天時我相我的
身体很好以後有我们可是有的
童把太相屈了因為教士你在家升
中能費到行的遠去常市教士嚴肅
吧把望氣著有力的家人也毫无我蠲志
沒有未教士的爱人也一去力逛吧
吧盼望氣我列在無天補造也了要為我教
世把是教士呈要的才打呀掌為教
士的等人補造我列如今還息教
士希望教士今年一定回來現在我

Translation of the letter from the previous page

Teacher Fei - Peace to you.

Teacher Fei, by now you must have seen the letter that I previously had sent to you. How has your health been recently? I'm sure all is well at home, but of course I cannot know for sure. I hope you will pray hard for me. Let me tell you about my circumstances here recently. My health has been good and I have not been sick, but my spirit is weak. When you were here I could always go over and pray often with you to gain strength. Now I have no strength left at all. I ask all of your family to pray for me. I hope that each time you pray, wou will not forget me. That's how you always helped me. And I will also pray for your family. Even now I still miss you and hope that this year you will return.

Ai Gwang and I still keep your house clean. Ai Gwang will soon go to Feng Tian (Zhu Tian?) to learn Obstetrics. I feel very bad, because I am just not as useful as other people - I can only stay at home. There isn;t even anything you can do for me.

During the Sho Chung Festival (harvest?) we had some pictures taken, and I wanted to give you one. You can see how much heavier I've become! We also gave Doctor Li a photo. I wanted to give you this picture because I thought you would certainly be happy to see how well all of us girls are doing here. We all wish you peace.

Best wishes to your family

Ai Zhen

his brother, Carl, owned a prospering business and had become millionaires! Wonders did not cease. I spent the night in Phoenix and had a great time sharing memories. I was told that some years later as George was dying, he said, "I can't wait to meet my Savior." I had always cared about him and had prayed for him for years!

Congregations welcome news of China mission work

I returned to L.A. with Sally and her husband. Throughout my trip, I spoke in various churches about the mission work in China. Pastors at the time seemed very eager to hear presentations on the subject. After I spoke at a church in L.A., a young Lutheran pastor presented me with a beautiful leather-bound Bible. I had been wanting an English version. I had one printed in Danish and one in Chinese, but none in English. This was a special gift and meant a lot to me. On the flyleaf Pastor Robertson wrote,

To Miss Dagmar Petersen with a prayer for God's rich and continued blessings upon your work. Jeremiah 31:3. G. J. Robertson, Los Angeles, California, Sept. 22, 1946.

I had another pleasant break in my cross-country train ride, when I stopped to visit my cousin, Albert Peterson, and his wife, Elva, in Denver, Colorado. Elva was a liberal arts teacher in the Women's College and had spent a year in Denmark while she attended Niels Buch's Gymnastic School. They introduced me to their church, their friends, and all the beautiful surrounding area, including an ice skating arena. It was in Denver where I met the Josephsons. They were a very interesting couple. Both were physicians. She was originally from Russia. He was from Cambridge, Wisconsin. Later I would learn that he had been confirmed in the church with my future husband, Joe Vasby, whom I had not yet met at this time. It really is a small world at times!

My next stop was in Omaha and Blair, Nebraska, where my father had spent eight years in college and seminary. There was still a large Danish community in this area, and to my delight, many people whom I met also knew my parents. I was invited to spend a week at Dana College, intermingling with the students and telling them about mission work in China. That was a very exciting week for me. I became acquainted with several old college friends of my father and heard stories about my parents that I had not known. Everyone spoke highly of them. For the first time I was walking on the same streets and visiting the tower in Old Main where my father had roomed. I could not believe it. I felt so close to my parents during this time. I gave talks about our work in China a few times in the surrounding area before moving on to Illinois.

In Illinois I visited in Chicago, Des Plaines, and Evanston where my uncle, P. M. Petersen, and my aunt had worked and lived for many years and where several of my cousins still worked. Ralph, my oldest cousin, was employed in the business office of Northwestern University. Evelyn, the youngest of the seven cousins from this family, was married while I was visiting. I was happy to be able to attend her wedding; I had missed all family events for almost a decade.

These Illinois cousins showed me the sights in the area and gave me a ride when I was asked to speak to a group of college students in Des Plaines. As I began my presentation to the students, I was appalled by their seeming apathy as they settled down casually with the lights lowered. Again I was experiencing culture shock. An education for many of these American students was something that was expected; it was their way of life. In Denmark, and especially in China, higher education was a rare opportunity which called for sacrifice and much effort on the part of the student and family involved. Students in these countries would have shown their interest and respect through more formal behavior. The contrast in behavior was striking.

Unknowingly visiting my future home

My next stop in my cross-country journey was Cambridge, Wisconsin, a small rural town in south central Wisconsin. My uncle, P. M. Petersen, and aunt, Bertine, had bought a house there in which to enjoy their retirement. P. M. had earlier served as the pastor of Willerup Methodist Church in Cambridge, the oldest Scandinavian Methodist Church in the world. At the time I never imagined that eight years later I would be married and would make my home in this town! While I met my future family during this visit, I did not yet know them well or even have an inkling how important these people would become to me.

In Cambridge, I met Ardelle Jarlsberg, a single woman who worked tirelessly on behalf of the church youth and mission programs. Ardelle was a sister-in-law to the man who would become my husband. Ardelle arranged speaking engagements for me and eagerly drove me around to them. One day she called to tell me that she had talked with the President of the Wisconsin Methodist Women's Association and had arranged for me to speak at their annual convention in Milwaukee. While they already had a full program planned for the day, they offered me a ten minute time slot. Following my few brief words, a kind woman who sat beside me dropped a check for $50 in my lap! The woman was Mrs. Chase from the Kohler Company. Later the Chases would donate a new generator for the work at Ganta Mission when I was stationed in Liberia.

In Racine, Wisconsin, I visited the Reverend and Mrs. Wilhelmsen of Gethsemane Lutheran Church; they were a dear couple who were friends of my parents. They invited me to speak at their church, and afterwards Pastor Wilhelmsen told the church synod that I should be given a wide hearing. This happened a year later.

Return to Trufant, Michigan

I made one more special visit in the U.S. While in Cambridge, I called a dear friend, Grace Vanderveen, who lived in Grand Rapids, Michigan. Grace and another woman, Louise Oasting, had been childhood friends with my sister, Marie, and me. They attended church in Trufant, Michigan, when my father was pastor there from 1911 to 1920. Louise and Grace were the daughters of some of our most faithful church members. Grace was a year older than Marie, and Louise was a year older than Grace, so the four of us were close in age and had much in common. We had kept in touch during the intervening years. Louise and Grace were both married and had lovely homes in Grand Rapids.

When I called, Grace happened to be outside working in her garden. A man was there painting her windows and heard the telephone. Knowing that she could not hear the phone, he let himself in, grabbed the phone, and called Grace. This was a fortuitous act, since at that time even long-distance phone calls were not a routine form of communication because of the cost.

When Grace heard my voice, she did not realize that I was in the States. She said, "Oh Dagmar, I am so excited. This morning I was thinking about you and your father. They have asked me to teach Sunday School, and I feel so incompetent. I was wishing that I could talk with you or your father." She quickly arranged for my visit by getting in touch with St. Thomas Church in Trufant. The church, in turn, arranged for a welcoming party and asked me to speak. What a wonderful surprise awaited me! I was welcomed by 100 people who had known my family and loved my father as their former pastor. As usual when I spoke, an offering was taken for the work of the mission.

My second view of the Statue of Liberty

Finally, I was approaching the last leg of my trip. I traveled to New York and boarded the Norwegian ocean liner that would take me home. Like most of the passengers, I lined up along the rail to wave good-bye. I had no one there to whom I could wave, but I was still eager to get a last glimpse of U.S. soil. Just like the first time I left the U.S., 24 years before, I thought this might be the last time I would see the country of my birth. I have lasting impressions of the hustle and bustle, the noise and smells, the tears and smiles as our ship pulled out. The gangplank was raised. Anyone who was not on board, would no longer have a chance to make it. Then the fog horn blew so loudly that I had to cover my ears. The ship slowly backed away from the pier, turned around, and glided out into the ocean. The Statue of Liberty and the tall skyscrapers, the last images to be seen, slipped steadily from view.

I settled down in my comfortable cabin and for the first time in six weeks had time to really contemplate life. Even though I had been eager to return to Denmark after an absence of nine years, I realized what a gift the past six weeks had been.

9

Homecoming

Those who hope in the Lord will renew their strength. They will soar on wings like eagles; they will run and not grow weary, they will walk and not be faint. Isaiah 40:31 (NIV).

The long-awaited day arrives

The nine days crossing the ocean, as always for me, were interrupted by three days of seasickness. After that, I began to focus on the upcoming meeting with my dear parents and family. I wondered what had transpired for each of them under Hitler's regime, and I tried to come to terms with the death of my sister, Ruth, who was the last person to wave good-bye to me in Copenhagen when I left in 1937.

The ship docked temporarily in Christiania (Oslo), then headed for Copenhagen. It is difficult to describe the feelings I had that last night on board. I could not sleep and instead paced back and forth on the deck most of the night. I thought about how my parents must have felt when they returned to Denmark in 1922 after a separation of 18 years from their parents. I could hardly wait for the reunion. The night was so very long.

Morning finally did come. November 11, 1946, was a gray fall day, but there on the pier it was aglow with the spirit of love. Mother and Dad and Marie had traveled to Copenhagen to greet me at the harbor. There they stood, eager to see me and yet controlled. My faithful, loving parents looked almost the same as when I last saw them in 1937, although the war years had taken their toll and the habitual sparkle in their eyes had dulled a bit. It was wonderful to give them big hugs once again. Marie, who had spent many years in Greece as a missionary, had returned to Denmark a year earlier. It was a relief for my parents to know that all of their children were now safely back in the fold.

Father, Niels Christian Petersen, 1940

We spent the night in Copenhagen. My parents stayed with my brother Richard and his family. Their apartment was too small for all of us, so Marie and I stayed with friends. Richard, who had been so mischievous as a child, was now a pastor in Copenhagen. While I was in China, he had married Alma, the daughter of a missionary couple, who had served in India. Richard and Alma had two small children at that time, a four-year-old boy and a little eight-month-old girl. Later they would have another son, who would become my godchild.

Our friends had rather tight quarters, so Marie and I shared a bedroom and a bed that night. I thought that I had undergone difficult times in China, but when Marie began to pour out her heart to me, I lay there weeping instead of sleeping as she shared the horrors she had witnessed in Greece.

Marie's experience in Greece

After World War I while we were yet teenagers, our parents were involved with Armenian mission work. Following the war, Christian Armenians who lived in Turkey experienced horrible persecution that drove them out of their country. Many were killed. Their story can be likened to that of the Jews during the Nazi occupation. Many of the Armenians landed in Greece where the Danish people came to their rescue. My parents sponsored two small girls while we still lived in the U.S. Over the years we heard much about them.

In 1937 Marie accepted a position working with these refugees in Greece. Her work was funded by a Danish mission society named Armenian Mission. She left in March, while I left for China in August of the same year. The mission outreach in Greece included evangelism as well as support for daily life. Part of Marie's job involved supervising the school that had been established to teach the girls handiwork. The Armenians were known for their beautiful laces and delicate embroidery, which were sold in Denmark to help support the refugees. Marie also supervised a soup kitchen to help feed the very poor. About 50,000 Armenians, living in a refugee camp, needed such assistance. In addition, she assumed the responsibility of mission treasurer. Her natural leadership ability and her child care training made her a very capable leader. She had very good Armenian co-workers who had been trained by the people who had established the mission in Greece.

In 1939 when war broke out, the Armenian Mission called Marie home to Denmark. Because of the grave danger in Greece, she was given the option to remain in Denmark, but she wanted to return to help the people whom she had learned to love. Knowing it would be difficult to send money in the upcoming years, the Armenian Mission gave Marie a large sum of money to carry with her for the continuation of the work. When she told me about that trip through Europe, we both marveled at how miraculously God had protected her. There were many borders to cross, and she would be expected to declare the money as she moved from country to country. God surely sent angels to protect her along the way. She was never asked to declare the money. Also amazing was that young German soldiers traveling in the same train compartment watched over her. One cold winter night she was afraid of missing her connection. The soldiers told her to go to sleep. She gave them her ticket, and they kept watch for her. While the train was delayed for some reason, the wheels froze to the tracks. The soldiers woke Marie and told her that she needed to get off and catch another train that would soon be ready to go on the side track. They shared their food with her, helped her off the train, and soon she was on her way once again.

During the following years all was chaos as different countries fought for power in Greece. First the Germans invaded, later the Italians, and finally the communists took over. As in China, this caused civil war between the partisans and the Greek army. Only Marie could provide the details of those years, and only God knows how she survived.

During this time, a young Armenian girl came to Marie. She seemed like a gift from God. Araksie had been adopted into a Danish family, who had been in Greece earlier. When the family returned to Denmark, Araksie stayed in Greece and France to work. She became proficient in Danish, Greek, Armenian, French, and English! Marie took Araksie in as a daughter and took care of all her needs. Later when Araksie became engaged and married a Christian Armenian, Marie arranged and paid for her wedding. Marie still had contact with Denmark through the Danish ambassador and his wife who stayed in Greece through the war. They became close friends with Marie and helped her with whatever she needed. Since communication channels were open with Denmark, Marie heard by mail that our sister Ruth had died. When Araksie's first little baby was born, she named the baby, Ruth, in memory of Marie's sister. Now Marie also had a "grandchild."

As in all other nations that were victimized by war, food became more and more scarce in Greece. Even water was rationed strictly. Many of the supplies in Athens where Marie lived were sent to Egypt to support the army there. Athens, a city of marble and stone, was very hot that summer. The worst famine in Greece's history at the time struck the city. This was the very hardest time for Marie. A thousand people died each day, literally falling in their tracks on the streets or in their homes. Marie could never shake the haunting memory of some of the incidents she witnessed. One of these occurred in a home where nearly all members of the family had died. Her assistant visited the home daily. Each day a young man would eagerly await a little food when his mother would go out to search for some. And each day, upon returning home, she would have to say, "There was no food today." The mother went out day after day with the same result. Like many others, the young man died. The International Red Cross was able to ship food in for several hundred people, but as it was distributed, there was never enough for everyone. As Marie sought guidance about the situation, she was told to give the food only to those who had the capability to survive. Witnessing these horrors left Marie scarred for life.

Even with the overwhelming demands Marie felt in Greece, she remembered me in her prayers. As we lay talking in the dark that first night together, she told me about a dream she had while in Greece. "One night I awoke and knew I had to get up and pray for you," she said. "I felt very strongly that you were in serious trouble. I started to pray for you and I saw an airplane falling to the ground over your head. As I continued to pray, I saw Jesus. He wore a belt which he took off and threw around you and pulled you to safety!" How powerful was the prayer chain that encircled the globe among our family!

When the war was finally over, Marie was very ill with amoebic dysentery, malaria, and malnutrition. She was placed on a stretcher and taken to a ship that sailed through mine-ridden waters back to Denmark. There was no advance notice to my family that Marie was on her way home. On the day that she arrived in Copenhagen, my parents were away from home with some of the family, when suddenly mother insisted they leave and return home, saying that Marie was coming. Mother had always had a sixth sense when it came to her family. So everyone hurried home in time to welcome Marie back. Illness left Marie very weak, and she was hospitalized. When she heard that I was coming home, she demanded to be released and accompanied Mother and Dad when they came to meet my ship.

Fresh off the field

The next day my parents, Marie, and I went on our way to Aarhus, the city where my parents chose to retire. Actually, they lived in Aabyhøj, a suburb of Aarhus. It was exciting for me to see the home they had purchased - the first and only home they had owned! I had been concerned for several years about what they would do after they retired. I had prayed earnestly that God would give them their own home. He had abundantly provided a villa for sale at a price they could afford. They had bought the home during the war when it had been sold for a much smaller sum than it was worth. The home was situated on a good-sized lot filled with fruit trees and shrubs, and there was plenty of space for flower and vegetable gardens which my parents had always had in other locations.

My sister, Helga, was unavailable the day of my homecoming - a disappointment for us both. Her mother-in-law had died that very day, and she was needed elsewhere. Helga had picked up the loose ends when both Marie and I had left for our mission stations. She had assumed some of our financial obligations and had kept in touch with our friends as if they were her own. She kept me posted with news from Denmark until communication links with China were sealed. In one of her letters that reached me before the mail was withheld she wrote, "I miss you so much, but it is good we can always be one in Spirit."

Helga was involved with Christian youth work in Copenhagen when she met her future husband, Ernst Frandsen, a businessman. On April 9, 1940, she, along with everyone else in Copenhagen, was caught up in the Nazi occupation. Rather unexpectedly the war planes came in hordes over Copenhagen, flying low and sending fear through everyone. Food was rationed and transportation became difficult. Helga and her family moved to Aarhus in 1946. At the time of my arrival, the first of their three sons had been born. The next two were twins. Since Helga was a dental technician, she felt very bad when she learned that I had lost some of my teeth and my four-tooth gold bridge while in China. She helped other people maintain their dental health every day; yet had not been able to help her own sister who lived so far away for nine years.

When Helga and I met for the first time after my arrival, she thought that I looked very nice in my new clothes but acknowledged that she had hoped to get a glimpse of me "fresh off the field!"

Other missionaries return from China

Gradually all but one of the Danish missionaries from Manchuria came home to Denmark as the communist rulers took over China step by step. Ellen Nielsen stayed there. Ellen had been one of the first missionaries to China, going there in the late 1800s. Her work drew much attention far and wide. She was one of my mother's favorites, and Mother had supported her work from the time it began. Ellen acquired Chinese citizenship so that she could buy land for her institution, which included a girls' boarding school, a teachers' college, and an industrial school. Her goal was to help the Chinese people become self-supporting citizens. With the communist take over, Ellen lost all that she had worked so hard to build. She would still not leave her beloved people. She was arrested and jailed for a period of time. In all, Ellen spent over 50 years of her life in China. She died at the age of 90 and was buried in China.

Ellen's right hand through many years was a teacher, Astrid Paulsen. Astrid was one of the 13 who walked out of China with me. She returned to China and was arrested and jailed along with Ellen Nielsen. Astrid made it back to Denmark to live out her days. She lived in a fifth floor apartment in a house in Aarhus that had belonged to her father. My family kept in touch with her, and I was able to meet with her when I was in town visiting my family. It was always a great experience to recall memories and to chat with her in Chinese. Eventually she lost her sight, but she continued to praise God. She lived to be 100 years old.

Karen Gormsen, who also had spent the best years of her life in China, had to leave her beloved orphans, her sick patients, and nurses. She had many nightmares about all the children she left behind. She did not live many years after she returned home to Denmark. She died, it was said, of a "broken heart."

Readjustment and Reacquaintance

When we arrived in Denmark, the little country that so recently had regained its freedom again, the scars of war were very evident. Shells of buildings that had been bombed were everywhere. Material goods such as food and clothing were scarce. Gasoline was being rationed, and transportation was disrupted. How would we, the returning missionaries, fit in with our needs for housing and jobs?

I was able to stay with my parents, sharing a small room with Marie. The highlight of this first year back home was getting acquainted with new members of the family - new in-laws and babies - and becoming reacquainted with my nieces and nephews, who had added nine years to their lives since I had last seen them. Our family had always been close-knit. The years of separation only added affection and appreciation for one another.

At the age of 20, my sister Esther had married a farmer, Christian Jensen, known to everyone as "Chris." Quiet and unassuming, Esther always kept her home open to others. She was a very good housekeeper, and her garden and home were full of flowers and plants. Her hands were never idle; she sewed, crocheted, knit, quilted, and made lace. Her work was always done to perfection. Esther and her husband eventually had five children, including two sets of twins. I became godmother to one girl and one boy.

Grace and Ruth both worked in London and Scotland for a year when they were young. Grace then moved to Holstebro, Denmark, where she worked as a nurse for many years until she married Wilfred Risgaard, a teacher, who was also an artist. His media were paint and pottery. Grace and her husband eventually had three children and were very active in mission work in Holstebro.

With sadness I learned more about the death of my sister Ruth and her life before she died. She had been one of the bright bookworms in our family. She could be found lying on the floor reading the paper or a book before she went to school. She was 23 years old and at the head of her class in college, ready to graduate with high honors in the spring and was engaged to a young man who attended the same college, when she died very unexpectedly of some complications following surgery. This was such a shock to everyone. She died in a hospital in Copenhagen. Mother and one of my sisters accompanied her body home on the train. My father stayed home to conduct the Christmas service at the church. Such was his dedication that despite the shock of Ruth's death and his grief, he continued to preach his sermon as the train pulled in close to the church!

Naomi, the youngest of my siblings, was only 16 when I left for China. Now when I returned, I learned about her life from her own stories and those of other family members. In school Naomi had been rather mischievous; she loved to play pranks and not get caught. When she graduated, she decided that she wanted to go to college and become a teacher. She explained that Dad did not believe she was serious and asked her to prove her sincerity. She took out a loan and went through a very arduous time, since she graduated during the German occupation.

During the war Naomi, like many Danish youths, was involved in the underground movement. One day when my parents had been out of town for some days, some young people concealed weapons in their basement. Naomi had continued to live with our parents. When she came home from the school where she was teaching, she asked the young adults to remove the weapons immediately. She did not want Dad and Mother involved in this endeavor. The weapons were then moved with a neighbor's permission to a shed in his yard. Homes in Aabyhøj generally were quite close together, but on the street where my parents lived were several villas which were almost identical and had large yards and good-sized tool sheds. The Nazis came to inspect the houses on my parents' street that night. Naomi and my parents were home when they realized that the house on the left of them was being searched. The families had developed secret codes in order to communicate with each other during such times. Naomi stood in the window, using the code to communicate to the family on the right that the police were coming. The house and shed on the left were thoroughly searched. When the search party came to my parents' home, Mother was the spokesperson. She knew nothing about the weapons and answered honestly that she had never had any. The house on the right was to be searched next. As everyone there prayed for protection, the house was searched, but the shed was missed. God had spared them all. This was just one of many critical moments in the lives of my family who had remained in Denmark during the war years.

How can I offer joy to others when I have not laughed in years?

All of us returning missionaries were still employed by the Mission Board. Our gracious mission friends faithfully supported us. There was a great need for information from us about those silent years under Hitler's occupation of Denmark and the Japanese and communist take-over of Manchuria. We were often asked to speak at churches and mission gatherings.

As the winter passed and summer drew near, plans were made for the many camps to reopen for the season. I recall vividly my reaction when asked to take responsibility for a girls' Bible camp located by the Atlantic Ocean. I refused because I felt that the young girls needed a time of freedom, joy, and fun. I could not give them that fun time. It seemed that I had not laughed in years. After I was asked for the third time to lead the camp, I agreed to be responsible for the Bible studies, if the mission would provide someone else to entertain the teenage girls. The mission agreed to this plan. A few days before the opening day of camp, I received the news that the woman who was slated to help me had become seriously ill and could not go! They sent another, rather inexperienced, woman to help. It was with much prayer that I prepared to go.

The one-week camp went by quickly. The weather was beautiful. The splashing of the ocean waves upon the shore seemed to have a soothing effect on all in attendance. There was such a spirit of oneness as we shared the Bible and time in prayer. All the girls responded to the gospel message. Individually they came to me - on occasion even at three o'clock in the morning. All told me of their problems and their need for prayer.

On the last full day of camp, my co-worker came to me and said, "We need to just have a fun day." I agreed, but I told her that I would be at the far end of the beach just in case someone needed to talk. She planned a day off with the girls; yet, gradually throughout the day every girl ended up with me, wanting to hear more about God and His word. Sunday noon we all were seated around the table. The youngest girl sat beside me. The girls shared the highlights of their week with each other. "Esther," I said, "What did you get out of this week's camp?" With joy in her answer, she said, "I asked Jesus into my heart." "When did you do that?" I asked. "Oh, just now," came her reply.

94

We exchanged addresses before we parted. In the fall the girls planned a reunion. I remember the date because it was my mother's 71st birthday. This time I knew that I could not leave my mother, as I had to do so often before. We still did not have cars, and the location of the reunion was several hours away. I asked to be excused, but my request was not accepted! Those precious girls rented a taxi and invited both of my parents along with me to share the day with them. We found that the girls had kept their commitments to Christ. We left the reunion with joyful hearts. My parents always put God's plan ahead of their own.

Return to the U.S.

As the year passed I experienced a sense of anticipation about what might lie ahead. I had received many invitations to return to the U.S. to visit friends and relatives and to speak at Lutheran churches. I approached the mission board about the idea. They agreed to the plan and offered to pay for my trip to the U.S. if I would support myself from there. This meant that the mission board would cease to pay my salary on a regular basis. If I obtained speaking engagements, I could keep my usual $100 monthly salary and would forward the remainder to the mission board.

Marie was still ill and very uncertain about her future. She felt that I was the only person who really understood her. Part of Marie's bond with me was based on feelings we both had that spies were following us and eavesdropping on our conversations. We felt that we were both under suspicion because of our previous work in communist controlled countries. Would there be repercussions from our mission work? It is hard to say to what extent our fears were justified. Were our experiences real or were they imagined, based upon years of such occurrences in the countries in which we had served? It was a help to Marie that I understood her fears of being followed and acknowledged that these incidents happened to me also.

When I decided to leave again for the U.S., Marie literally became very ill. I knew that she needed to get away from the memories of famine and death that haunted her from the war years in Greece. I invited her to go with me, and the Lord made it possible for the two of us to travel to the U.S. together.

A doll helps Marie heal

Two homes became available to us in Wisconsin. The first was the home of our uncle, the Rev. P.M. Petersen, in Cambridge, Wisconsin. Our second welcome came from Mr. and Mrs. Bidstrup in Racine, Wisconsin, who were friends of my mother. Mr. Bidstrup's parents had been neighbors of my mother's parents in Denmark, when mother was a young girl. The Bidstrups had only one child, a daughter, who had died in an auto accident at the age of 18. The couple were glad to have us live with them for five months to help fill the empty space left by the death of their beloved daughter.

From these two home bases, Marie and I traveled together for six months.

Marie spoke about her time in Greece and her work with the Red Cross, the organization that made it possible for her to carry out her work during those very hard years. I, of course, shared my experiences in Manchuria. Before Marie returned to Denmark, the friends of Willerup Methodist Church, in Cambridge, Wisconsin, had a shower for us. The shower provided us with items to use in our mission work. Previously Marie had shared a wish with me that she could get a doll to send to her precious "granddaughter" in Greece. My uncle felt that buying a doll with our mission salaries when there were so many other needs was inappropriate. I had told Marie that I would find a doll - we would ask God to get one for her before she returned to Denmark. A neighbor and friend of my uncle hosted the shower. We received many beautiful and useful things to use for our mission projects, mostly baby and children's clothing. Amidst all the beautiful and useful things we received was a doll! The doll had been donated by Ruth Kenseth. In memory of our sister Ruth, who had died so young, we named the doll Ruth and sent it to Greece for little Ruth. The doll seems like such a small thing, but it proved to be a real healing experience for Marie.

God provides for Ardelle's mother

After Marie left, I remained in the U.S. for another six months. Ardelle Jarlsberg, my friend from Cambridge, Wisconsin, who was an avid supporter of missions, came to me one day and suggested that we go west to California on a speaking tour. She loved to drive. I remember answering her that we could go if she had faith. I had no money to finance the trip, but I knew that the Lord would provide for us if the trip was His will. I wondered, though, how Ardelle could leave her widowed mother to make the trip. Again, I knew of only one way to ensure her mother's well-being. I prayed that God would provide for Ardelle's mother so that she would have no needs as we left on the trip.

In the meantime I was invited to speak at a youth rally held in a Minnesota church. The invitation was extended by the brother of the Rev. Borge, the pastor of a church in Rockdale, Wisconsin, a close neighbor to Cambridge. A sizable group attended the rally in Minnesota. I made it a practice never to ask for money during speaking engagements. I would describe the mission work and also share the Gospel without referring in any way to finances. I felt that this was a very important principle to follow. I wanted to trust God alone for our needs, and I wanted to maintain the trust and confidence of the wonderful people who supported the missions and the church. I also refused to handle any money that was donated for mission work. Whenever someone offered money for the support of the missions, I requested that the money be sent directly to the mission office. While I was in the U.S., my finances were handled through a representative from our mission located in Des Moines, Iowa. The Minnesota group, however, presented me with $72, the results of a freewill offering. They gave it directly to me stipulating that this money was a personal gift and not for the mission work. I took the money back to Wisconsin and gave it all to Ardelle's mother for her to use while she was alone. With the financial worries for Ardelle's mother behind us, we started across the U.S., visiting cousins and churches as opportunities presented themselves. God opened more doors than we had ever hoped. After some months we had covered many thousands of miles.

Destination not China, but Africa

During this time, I had also been searching for a way to return to China. This dream was not meant to be. While Ardelle and I were in California, I received a letter from the president of our mission board in Denmark asking me to go to New York to visit different mission boards there. An international conference had been held in Amsterdam. Disruption of mission work and changes for missions had been on the agenda. Several American missions were in need of workers and had offered to support Danish missionaries whose work had been disrupted by the war. The first board that I sought out in New York was the Board of Missions of the Methodist Church in the U.S. Dr. Harold Brewster, the president of the board, interviewed me for an hour. He then described three available opportunities for me. I could go to Tanzania, the Congo, or Ganta Mission in Liberia. As he was explaining the different mission possibilities, a voice within me kept saying, "Ganta Mission. Ganta Mission." When he was finished, I immediately told him that I would go to Ganta, Liberia. He looked at me for a moment and said, "Now, I have tried for an hour to explain to you that Ganta is a very difficult mission, and yet you chose Ganta! Why?" Maybe part of the reason for my decision was that English is the official language of Liberia, and if I went there I would not need to learn another language. Yet, I could not fully explain why my mind was set on Ganta Mission.

Dr. Brewster was eager to send me off to Liberia at once. I told him that I needed to go back to Denmark. It was late fall. I needed to see my parents and my own mission board. I also wanted to celebrate Christmas with my parents. I was so happy to have this prospect of continuing my missionary work. Interestingly, in my heart, I had often wished to visit Africa.

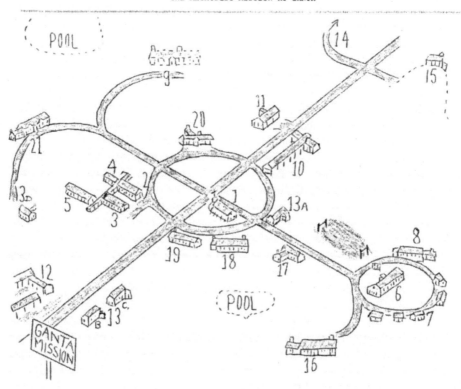

The Methodist Mission at Ganta

1. Church
2. Clinic
3. Wards
4. Hospital
5. Service Wing
6. School
7. Dormitories
8. Dinning Hall
9. Hostel for Girls
10. Saw Mill and Carpenter Shop
11. Garage and Machine Shop
12. Tile Brick Yard

13a. Liberian Staff House
13b. Liberian Staff House
13c. Liberian Staff House
13d. Liberian Staff House
14. To Leprosy Colony
15. Hill House
16. Cofield House
17. Haffen House
18. Mission House
19. Mission House
20. The Stone House - Dr. Harley
21. Nurses House

98

10

Ganta Mission
Liberia

The Lord will keep you from all harm - he will watch over your life; the Lord will watch over your coming and going both now and forevermore. Psalm 121:7-8 (NIV).

Have I made the right decision?

My mission board was happy to be able to "loan" me out to the Board of Missions of the Methodist Church in the U.S. Preparing to launch out once more for an unknown mission left me in the same sort of fuzzy period I had experienced when I prepared to go to China more than a decade earlier. The days passed quickly with a sort of whipped up frenzy of activities - correspondence with the mission boards, physical check-ups, shots, passports, visas, obtaining clothes suitable for the tropics, and travelling around Denmark to meet with supporters. Last, but not least, were the farewells once again to my family.

Since it was only a couple of years since the war had ceased, Europe was still in ruins. This meant that making transportation reservations was difficult and time-consuming. I was booked on a Dutch ocean liner out of Bordeaux, France, because it was scheduled to sail directly to the port city of Monrovia, Liberia. I left Copenhagen in early March, 1949. Before I left, I completed some last minute shopping and took a bus to get some medication for my skin at The Finsens Institute, which was established by Niels Ryberg Finsen, a Danish scientist and physician who was awarded the Nobel prize in Medicine in

1903 for his use of ultraviolet light rays to treat diseases such as lupus. While in China I had developed a rash which flared up from time to time. I stood on a street corner for a long time waiting for the bus to take me to the institute. The weather was bitterly cold with a strong wind that always seems to blow in Denmark. I felt the wind cutting into my sensitive face. Later as I boarded the train for Paris/Bordeaux, I applied the newly prescribed salve to my face and assumed it would heal shortly.

The train went through Amsterdam with a layover in Paris. It was rather a depressing ride, viewing all the bombed out buildings. Two young Armenian men who were friends of my sister, Marie, met me at the station in Paris. She knew them from her years in Greece during the war. The men took me sightseeing in Paris in the afternoon and at night treated me to a sumptuous dinner at a fine seafood restaurant. I then boarded the train for Bordeaux and went to sleep in the sleeper car to get a much needed rest. That evening I became violently ill with food poisoning which kept me up all night with sieges of vomiting and diarrhea. I was left physically drained and a little worried. When day arrived, I wobbled out to the ship in the harbor, only to be told that we would not be sailing for another five days because the ship's interior was being painted. I was sent to a hotel where I stayed overnight. At that time after the war, travelers were allowed to take only $50 out of Denmark. I did not have enough money for four more nights of hotel charges. I went back to the ship and explained my plight to the captain and asked for permission to stay on board ship. He granted my request, and I was assigned to a newly painted cabin. The heat, the paint smell, lack of air circulation, and my weakened condition caused me to become nauseated all over again. My skin condition also began to show signs of more irritation. I prayed, "Lord, am I on the right track?" I wondered if Ganta Mission was the right plan for me. During the next few days I had no one with whom I could talk and no money to spend, so there was not much I could do. I kept telling myself that I needed to remain calm and quit worrying. Of course, I prayed about my situation daily. On the fifth day we sailed, and I finally felt better.

The ship stopped at Dakar, Senegal, for five days to unload cement. It was hot, and I did not want to go too far alone, so I stayed on ship. The cement dust was impossible to avoid; it was really irritating my skin, and I was now developing infection in the broken skin. There was no one whom I could consult and nothing to do but wait, pray, and trust. As the ship set sail once more, the captain announced that we would not be docking in Monrovia as planned. Instead I would need to get off in Sierra Leone! Now my patience was stretched to the limit. I told the captain that I had booked on that particular boat because it was scheduled to go directly to Monrovia. Further, I said that since I was allowed to carry so very little money out of Denmark, they would have to wire Denmark for more money or put me up somehow. I tried to thank God continually, but it was a struggle. If I had not been ill, I could have handled it better, but the thought of being a burden to anyone was very humbling. Perhaps that was the lesson I needed to learn. There was no harbor in Freetown,

Sierra Leone, at that time, so I was lowered into a small boat with my trunks and suitcases and transported to shore. All the time I was wondering where they would put me up. Someone telephoned a missionary couple in the area, and they came to get me. No one seemed to know when there would be passage out of Sierra Leone. I was told it could take up to six months! The mission was short one worker since one of the missionaries was in Monrovia giving birth to her baby. How could I impose on strangers who were already short-staffed and give them even more work? I have often wondered how it felt to the missionary couple to have such an unexpected visitor; they took good care of me for two days. Unexpectedly an English passenger liner arrived on the third day. I was off to Monrovia in style and comfort. Amazingly, the missionary couple who had rescued me, retired later in Janesville, Wisconsin, near Cambridge where eventually I would make my home, and I was able to visit with them there years later.

The next day I arrived in Monrovia and was greeted enthusiastically by a red-headed young man with a wide grin. His name was Charles Britt; everyone called him "Britt." He was an American minister working as a missionary at Ganta. "Here's the nurse we have been waiting and praying for, for a long time," he said. I had a sinking feeling in my stomach and was red-faced in more than one respect. I was thoroughly embarrassed to be "loaned" out to someone needing my help, looking and feeling as I did. "Here's the nurse," I thought, "who is in need of a doctor herself."

I stayed in a mission building in Monrovia with Susan Mitchell, a single woman who was a teacher at the college. She had adopted and raised several African children. A little seven-year-old girl still lived at home with her. The two-story house was encircled by a veranda, and I was given a room with one small window that opened up onto the porch. That section of the porch was enclosed and provided living quarters for rabbits and chickens. The weather was very hot, since we were near the equator, and the air was polluted with the smell of animal excrement. During the day, the little seven-year-old girl stayed home from school and would look in on me to see if I needed anything and bring me fresh water. I did not like to have her see me with a rash all over my face, but she helped stem my loneliness. Her sweet way of caring was a wonderful introduction to the children of Liberia. I developed a love for her that lasted for years and still gives me a comforting assurance of God's love.

I was introduced to a Lebanese doctor, who was very kind and caring, and treated me as best he could. Two weeks passed without any change in my condition. I was given autoblood as a last resort. This consisted of having my own blood drawn and then re-injected. At the time, it was a procedure used when other treatments failed. Finally one night at 11:00 P.M., I could stand it no longer. I got up, left the house quietly, and walked several blocks to the doctor's house. I told him that I was at my wit's end. He then said, "You are a missionary, aren't you? You pray, don't you?" I could only answer, "Yes." Then he said that I could either go back to Denmark or travel on to Ganta Mission. "Sometimes a change of climate helps people," he remarked. Natu-

Bridge from Monrovia to Ganta Mission

rally I was wondering why this had happened and whether I had made the wrong decision to come to Liberia. I did not think so. The next day I contacted Britt, who had been waiting for me in Monrovia, and we made plans to complete the journey to Ganta Mission. When I was riding in the car with him that day, we met a car containing several Swedish missionaries. They did not see me in the car, but I heard them ask Britt, "How is your new missionary doing? Tell her we are praying for her." How good their concern felt - offered for someone whom they did not even know. I was reminded that all along my guidance had been to go to Ganta, so it could not be the right choice to give up and return to Denmark.

Britt had been busily gathering supplies for Ganta Mission. The red pickup truck was loaded down as we set out. It was common practice to take on local passengers who needed rides. They would climb up and perch on bags of rice or other goods. Only a short portion of the 175 mile trip to Ganta was paved at that time. We needed to cross rivers and streams in several places where the bridges consisted of a variety of boards and planks laid down with a good deal of space between them. The missionaries became rather adept at maneuvering their vehicles across these loose contraptions. Some of them seemed quite risky to me. If the loads were too heavy, the passengers would all scramble out and walk across the bridge.

Healing helps forge a bond with Dr. Harley

I arrived during the dry season when the roads were covered in red dust. For the entire trip, which took the better part of a day, I held my handkerchief over my face for protection. It was evening as we drove into the village of Ganta. A bright moon shone down on the round straw huts clumped together.

102

There was no grass, but the grounds were swept clean. A few lights flickered here and there, like stars that had fallen out of the sky and had landed in that unique landscape. In some places the smoke from the cooking fires rose into the entirely quiet and still evening. It seemed a little eerie to me at first, and I wondered how I would ever fit in. It was so different from any place I had lived before. "Oh, well," I thought, "Others have survived, so will you." After another few miles down the road, we entered a gate; a sign above told me it was "Ganta Mission."

I was installed in the Haffen House with Mildred Black. The house consisted of two small bedrooms, a small living/dining room connected to the kitchen by a screened-in breezeway, and a small bathroom. There was no running water and few other conveniences. The only utility that reminded me of our kitchen back home was a refrigerator cooled by a system using kerosene. Electricity was available only four hours in the evening.

Mildred greeted me very graciously and did not appear too shocked by my red face. Word was sent to Dr. George Harley, the founder of Ganta Mission, that I had arrived, and he came over to welcome me. I was so embarrassed by my physical condition, tired, and humbled, that I apologized for being there! That night I could not obtain any impression whatsoever of Dr. Harley, who spoke very little and gave me a penetrating look. He just told me to take a mercurochrome bath ("Whatever that is," I thought.) and to cover my face with a paste of saturated epsom salts. On that note he left Mildred to help me with his seemingly strange orders.

Quite early the next morning, Dr. Harley came again. This time he sat down, apologized for his abrupt behavior the previous evening, and for some inexplicable reason, poured out his heart to me on many things. He seemed quite discouraged. He had recently come back from a furlough to the States and was very disappointed by the lack of understanding and funds he had received regarding his great dreams for Ganta Mission. He also explained to me that many highly educated people could not understand his own, sometimes unconventional cures, one of which was his strong use of epsom salts. I was happy to tell him that I was feeling better already. In fact, on the third day of Dr. Harley's prescribed treatment, I was completely healed. I maintained perfectly healthy skin for the next three years of my service at Ganta Mission! This healing incident was instrumental in bringing about an excellent working relationship with Dr. Harley, one that I profited much by in our work together.

I become the first nurse at Ganta Mission

With the healing of my skin, I became re-energized and felt truly ready to get to work. Dr. Harley told me that I was his first nurse and that I should go ahead and make any changes that I wanted. The mission had been in existence almost 25 years. Of course, I knew that it would be foolish for me to come in with my own ideas when the other missionaries had established the work in the best possible way. The clinic helped a tremendous number of people but

Dagmar with Dr. Harley's four assistants

had very little equipment or supplies. Patients were scheduled to come in on certain days of the week. Two days a week people lined up for yaws treatment. Yaws, which was very prevalent, is a tropical disease caused by a spirochete. It begins with a skin lesion and if left untreated can eventually destroy the bones and joints. People contracted it through contact with infected persons, their clothing, or insects. Walking barefoot, it was believed, contributed to the transmission of the disease. Treatment consisted of injections of a drug containing arsenic. Later when tetramycin was developed, the disease responded to this antibiotic. One day a week, patients with Trypanasoma, sleeping sickness caused by the bite of a tsetse fly, were treated with injections of tryparsamide, another drug containing arsenic. On two other days of the week, people with bowel and stomach ailments would line up with stool specimens.

Dr. Harley's lovely wife, Winifred, was trained to do the lab work. Mildred Black, an American missionary who had assisted Dr. Harley almost from the beginning of his practice, gave intervenous injections and helped with almost everything else. Dr. Harley trained four young Liberian men to help with the injections and treatments. One of the young men had been a medic in the British army. One school girl and several school boys, who were interested in the medical work, assisted with many tasks. I was amazed at the efficient care given to so many patients. Some days 200 or more patients stood in line for shots!

Mildred, Winifred, or other available missionaries would be stationed at

104

the desk to dole out medicine, which was paid for with a very small amount of cash or other commodities. It was important for the patients to pay for their medication. This helped them understand the value of it and also kept the clinic operating. Each patient was given a ticket which was a tag about two inches by three inches used for identification and containing information for the staff. Most of the patients could not read, but symbols on the tickets helped them distinguish between the tickets of family members. Tickets for females had three signs, and the ones for males had four signs. Although Mano was the language spoken by most of the patients, people came to the clinic speaking many other dialects as well. Communication was very good with all the patients thanks to Frank Dimmerson, a Liberian who had worked with Dr. Harley for many years and who was proficient in several languages. He was our translator and was known to all as "Old Man Frank."

The clinic was a large room with bare cement floors and walls; there were windows on both sides. The windows were just screens with shutters that could be closed when rains or storms made it necessary to do so. A long porch stretched across the front entryway; this was where patients waited until they could be seen by the clinical staff. The back entrance opened onto a closed-in walkway which led to the laboratory and a utility area. Off one side of the clinic were three rooms. The largest of the three had been the original laboratory, but it was located on the west side and proved to be too hot for that purpose as the afternoon sun baked down on the building. Two other rooms were used for patients who needed beds. These rooms also had cement floors and walls. Each room contained one bed, which was used only in emergencies.

An oasis in the bush

In addition to the clinic, the mission compound contained a school house that met the educational needs of about 100 children, most of them boarding school students. Several Liberian teachers and missionaries taught in the school. Above the school was a large attic that served as a chapel and an auditorium for school plays. The benches were all alike, built of plain unpainted wood. A stage was located in the front of the room for performances. The compound contained many other buildings as well - a garage for mechanics to work and boys to learn the trade, a carpenter shop, a pottery shop, and several homes for the missionaries and Liberian teachers who lived in the compound. Seen from the sky, the mission was laid out in the form of a huge cross. The roads running lengthwise and crosswise were lined with mango and palm trees. At the lower half of the cross was a circle of houses and trees. Winifred Harley was a botanist, and Dr. Harley was also very interested in plants and flowers. Winifred specialized in ferns, and Dr. Harley in orchids. The place was beautiful! It is hard to imagine all of the love and labor that had turned this bush area into such a lovely spot that encompassed education, healing, employment, and worship for many thousands of people who passed through over the years. The mission had become a real oasis in the interior.

Patients at Ganta mission waiting for treatment
Mildred Black in foreground

Leper Colony in 1952

106

About two miles from the compound was a leprosy colony. Once a week one of the staff would go to the colony with our Liberian assistants to give painful shots of chaulmoogra oil, the only available treatment at the time. How good it was a few years later when new drugs became available that could be administered orally; however, this did not occur during my time in Africa.

Where will I fit in?

Ganta was known for the hospitality it offered for visitors of all kinds, who came to visit missions or were passing through on the main artery from Monrovia into the interior. In these surroundings I was left to try to figure out where I could fit in and how to go about establishing my little contribution to the hard-working staff. I loved the challenge that greeted me. Dr. Harley was gone much of the time to help when the government needed him to survey roads. Yet Dr. Harley was always ready to help me. If he could not be with a patient, he would give me good advice. I felt very close to the missionary staff almost immediately and believed that together we could do something worthwhile. I looked around and prayed for God to lead me every day. The years in China had given me experience that would be useful in many areas. But, oh! There was so much that I did not know!

I have a hard time describing those first months. Many times I was needed for everything. Fortunately I had brought a new bicycle with me for transportation around the mission compound. I concentrated first on getting people together for morning devotions which was no problem. The people who worked in the laboratory (who were the senior staff), the translator, the laundry boys, cooks, and the school girls and boys attended faithfully. In regard to our medical mission, we continued to follow the clinic procedures which were well established from previous years of service. I learned much from the staff, and I observed and took notes. One critical need I tackled was sterilizing. The staff already did that in small boilers or kerosene burners, but these procedures needed to be improved. As the number of surgeries performed increased, so too did the need for items requiring sterilization. Patients needing emergency treatment and pregnant women about to deliver came in regularly. Whenever I had the time, I made bandages and sterile packs. I soon saw a need for setting up one room to handle emergencies. I took inventory of the supplies and equipment in the large room above the clinic and located some instruments that had been left behind by the army and donated to the hospital. I found an available cupboard and sorted through the instruments. Another area of service was caring for the school children who had so many needs. It took all of us to keep an eye on them.

Again, I need medical care

When I had been at Ganta Mission for just a few months, I noticed a small growth in my mouth. It seemed to slowly increase in size. I showed it to Dr.

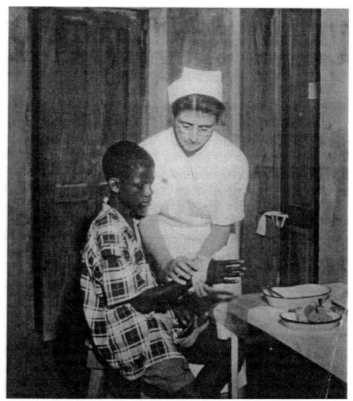

Dagmar treating a patient at Ganta Mission

Dagmar traveling to work at Ganta Mission, 1950

108

Harley and asked him to remove it. He did not respond at all. So, I went about my business, thinking that the spot was nothing to worry about. A few days later he sent for me while I was in the midst of delivering a baby. When I went to find Dr. Harley, he told me that he was going to the Firestone Rubber Plantation that afternoon and wanted me to go with him to consult one of their doctors. I was kept in the hospital for a few days. When the tests were completed, I was told that I would have to go home to have the growth removed. It could be malignant.

I was more puzzled than ever about my service to Ganta. I knew that God had a plan; I just did not know what it was. I returned to Ganta, packed up a few belongings, and was on my way again. I had the option of going to Denmark or the United States for surgery. I resisted the temptation to go home to see my family because it seemed more reasonable that I go to New York, since it was an American mission board that had hired me. My plane stopped in Paris for a short lay over. I called my parents in Denmark. They were very surprised to learn where I was and why. I told them that God had a plan for me, and I knew that the surgery was not the only reason that I was going to New York.

I was sent to Prince George Hotel in New York where missionaries in transit often stayed. With trepidation I contacted the mission board. What kind of help was I to Ganta anyway? Again, I was pleasantly surprised by the understanding and care I received.

The first Sunday in New York while I waited for my tests, I went down to the hotel lobby to look at a directory to see where I could go to church to worship. There was a Methodist church eight to ten blocks away. This seemed like a good choice since I now was a Methodist missionary. I set off early enough to walk to the church. On my way, I passed the Marble Collegiate Church. I felt led to stop there, but reasoned that I was headed for the Methodist church, and so I walked on. About halfway to the Methodist church, I could not rid myself of the feeling that I should turn back and attend the service at the Marble Collegiate Church. I turned around, went back to that church, and took a seat in the rear of the sanctuary. I looked around to identify some special reason why I was there. A few seats ahead of me, I saw two Chinese women, who reminded me so much of the Chinese Bible Women with whom I had worked. I settled down to follow the service, thinking that perhaps I would meet these women. When the service ended and I stepped out the door, I ran into Rosalind Rinker, who had befriended me when I was a student in Peking! We chatted, and she introduced me to the Chinese women. Then Rosalind introduced me to a young lady, Mary Nell Harper, who was also staying at the Prince George Hotel. We had actually ridden in the elevator together! When Mary learned that I was a missionary, she told me that she was on her way to Abyssinia (now Ethiopia) as a missionary. For some reason she had been detained in New York and was very lonely. Mary and I spent the next week in fellowship. She was so happy to meet an experienced missionary, and we had a prayer session daily as there was opportunity to do so.

Following my surgery I came down with a fever, a cold and a strong nose-bleed. It was a very strange, lonely time for me. As I read my Bible, I was reminded several times, "Just pray!" I knew there was much to pray about - the outcome of the surgery, the work I had left behind, and what possibly I would be doing next! Great was my relief when the report came that the little tumor was benign! I went to the mission office to report the good news to Dr. Brewster. During the visit I was asked what I thought about the work at Ganta and what prospects were there for the future. I understood that some people thought too much money had gone into too many projects without sufficient results. I told the mission administration that they should do all they could to support Dr. Harley in his work, that he was a unique man with insight and all he needed was help. Dr. Brewster said, "Well, now you can go right back to Ganta, or you can stay a while in this country - but that would be on your own." He meant that I would be responsible for my own support during the time I remained in the U.S. I decided to think about the options for another day. That evening I received a telephone call from my friend, Ardelle Jarlsberg, in Cambridge, Wisconsin. When she heard the test results, she said, "If you can stay, I will come to New York to get you." I spoke with Dr. Brewster about her offer the next day. He said, "We will take that as a sign that you should stay a few months."

The reason for my trip to the U.S.

True to her word, Ardelle arrived in New York as soon as she could get there. Early on Sunday morning we were on the road headed to Cambridge, Wisconsin. When we traveled together on Sundays, we usually stopped at a nearby church to worship. This time Ardelle did not mention where we were going before we were almost there. Then she asked if it was all right with me if we worshipped at the Memorial Baptist Church; it was north of New York in Poughkeepsie. The Reverend Alan Knight was the pastor of the church; he was married to Pearl Prescott of Cambridge, Wisconsin. I, of course, was happy to visit this church. I asked Ardelle, however, not to mention that I was there. She did not answer, so I sat back to enjoy the service. My request may seem strange to those who are not familiar with mission culture, but a missionary is always asked to give a "little greeting" from the mission field when travelling. I was tired and this time wanted to avoid public speaking. My wish was not granted, however. As the Reverend Knight came to the pulpit, he announced that a missionary was visiting this morning. Then he turned to me where I was sitting in the back of the church and said, "Dagmar, would you bring a little greeting from Liberia?" How Ardelle had gotten a message to Pastor Knight, I never knew. I had no choice but to march up front to the pulpit. He whispered to me, "You can take ten minutes." Quickly I sent a prayer up for wisdom to bring the right message. Just as I was about to speak, Pastor Knight whispered again, "You are on the air!" My impromptu message was being broadcast!

110

I had no time to worry or wonder. I began my short "sermonette" by describing my "rush hour" experiences in New York. From there, I described "rush hour" in the work of a mission; the needs were so great. One thing I had in mind was the long line of children who wanted to go to school at Ganta and the lack of materials and room for them. Bibles were one of our great needs in the mission. True to His promises, the Lord always provides for all our needs. An offering was taken for the work of the mission, and 100 Bibles were sent later from radio listeners. This experience was a very encouraging start to a four-month stay in the States.

I stayed with Ardelle and her mother in Cambridge, Wisconsin. As she had done in the past, Ardelle offered her time, her car, and her gift of love for missions. She arranged many speaking opportunities. Between contacts with relatives and friends, we covered many miles. My list of contacts had grown when the missionaries in Ganta had given me addresses of their friends and relatives in Oklahoma and Florida. One trip took Ardelle and me to Florida where we visited the home of William Cofield, the brother of a fellow Ganta missionary, B. B. Cofield. At this time, William was the chaplain for the state prison in Florida. He asked me to speak to the 700 inmates. It was wonderful to bring the message of God's love to them. In the morning there was also an opportunity to partake in the morning devotional period at the prison One of the inmates presented me with a model of a horse drawn carriage, which was made of little insignificant materials. I was told these models were made for use in Hollywood movies. The Cofields became dear friends of mine for life.

After four months of speaking engagements, I felt ready to return to Liberia. I had received monetary gifts totalling $749.95. In 1949 this was a large sum of money and purchased many needed items for the mission. I returned with plastic and rubber sheeting, scales to weigh babies, and a large scale for children and adults, test tubes for the lab, second-hand nursing books, physiology and anatomy charts, clocks, material for uniforms, paint for the surgical area, streptomycin for a boy with tuberculosis, vitamins, medical books, song books, and bible pictures. Twenty beds, slated for the new hospital which was being built, were donated by the Willerup Methodist Sunday School in Cambridge, Wisconsin, through the inspiration and support of their superintendent, Don Prescott, who owned a furniture store. (Before we moved into the hospital, a visitor from the philanthropic American Mellon family saw our need for mattresses for the beds and donated them.) The women of this church also sewed 100 brown pants and shirts for the girls and boys of the Ganta Mission School. They added beautiful yellow tee shirts to complete the uniforms. Later the church sent 30 pillows for the hospital beds. The Chase family of Kohler, Wisconsin, sent a generator for the mission station; this improved the dispensing of much needed electricity.

Although busy, my four months in the U.S. were wonderful, restful, and a time of miracles. The support I had received was astounding! This time I left for Liberia with great expectations. My friends, Ardelle Jarlsberg and Grace Vanderveen from Grand Rapids, Michigan, took me cross country by car to

*Ganta Mission School students dressed in new outfits provided
by Willerup Methodist Church, Cambridge, Wisconsin*

Port Arthur, Texas, where we spent a couple days before the ship to Liberia left the port. The week on board was restful and uneventful, although I did experience a scary incident one evening at dinner. A fish bone lodged crosswise in my throat and would not budge. I had to leave the table. I recall praying, "God, no one else can help me with this." The bone finally dislodged, and I was reminded again of God's wonderful care for all the details of His children's lives. The ship docked in Haiti for a day while in route. During the journey I became good friends with a couple of women missionaries from the Assembly of God denomination.

This time when I arrived in Monrovia, it was with great anticipation. Dr. Harley was there to pick me up. He arrived in a "new" car - a well-used Cadillac. The road had been improved since my first trip to Monrovia. This was in large part thanks to Dr. Harley's input and efforts; he became involved in any project that benefitted the people of Liberia. We were still several miles from Ganta in the early evening when our wonderful "new" car decided that it would go no further. Dr. Harley, who was so efficient with all tasks, could not repair it. Darkness was closing in, and we were close to the forest. I did not know what we would do next. Certainly I was not a great help, except that I could pray. Dr. Harley offered two choices. We could leave the car and walk to the next village, which was at least an hour away, or I could stay with the car and he would walk to get help. I decided to stay with the car. I felt so sorry for Dr. Harley as he walked off. One has to experience a dark tropical night to know how he must have felt. It was good that I had experienced many difficult situations over the years, since I was now in another rather unnerving one. The

112

forest close by was filled with night sounds - birds and other animals either getting ready to sleep or to kill their prey. I locked the doors and was totally alone. I had no idea when Dr. Harley would get back or if he would. We knew that this was the time of year when the heart hunters were prowling. Superstition at the time taught that if someone obtained a live human heart, he would be granted a promotion to some office. Again, the Lord was near. I felt at perfect peace and tried to sleep. Several hours later, Dr. Harley returned with some local help, and we were on our way again.

What a difference it made returning to someone who knew me and appreciated my work, compared to my first embarrassing arrival at Ganta Mission! Also, what joy there was in sharing with the staff the many donated items that would be so critical in our continued work. Obtaining these needed supplies, I thought, was the "real" reason that I had been sent to New York. I could hardly wait to get started! Every item I brought back was soon put to good use. The school children were so proud and happy when they received their new uniforms, and their morale was boosted. By some miracle, each one received a well-fitting uniform, even though I had not obtained sizes or even anticipated this need upon my departure from Ganta!

Organizing the clinic

Gradually I was able to organize the clinic. I started by setting up a room where surgical procedures could be performed. B. B. Cofield was right there to help me. Originally the ceiling of the surgical area consisted of boards that also served as a floor to the attic above, where medical supplies were stored. Dust fell through the boards into the room below. Soon a new ceiling was installed, and the room was brightened and cleansed by the green paint which had been purchased in the far away lumber yard in Cambridge, Wisconsin. I added new supplies to the instrument cupboard that I had started before I had left for the States. There was new fabric for sheets and bandages. Before long, emergencies were handled in this renovated room.

The next room I tackled was the room that had been the first laboratory. We converted this room to use for morning devotions, clinical instruction, and bandage-making. We painted the walls and benches green; then I hung a picture of Christ from the Prescott furniture store in Cambridge, Wisconsin. On the night of Maundy Thursday, all the preparations were finished, and the room was clean and fresh. After I hung the picture in place, I sat down on a bench and looked at that image of compassion and love. I then knelt down on the cement floor and prayed for God's blessing on the room. As I knelt, the thought came to me that I should ask Dr. Harley to lead our morning devotions on Good Friday. I hurried to his home and found him on the porch working on his specimen collection. My request seemed to take him by surprise. It seemed so long before he even looked up that I wondered if he would. He finally looked up at me with sorrowful eyes and said, "Dagmar, I have wished for so long that someone would ask me." The next morning he gave a very inspiring

Dagmar in Africa in 1950

message, and all of us left quietly filled with a new challenge.

Dr. Harley was a very unique man with an inquiring mind. He saw his mission as improving the living situation of the Liberian people. He was a scientist and researcher. I cannot begin to adequately explain his work that spanned 34 years, but it encompassed clinical practice, medical research, healing plants, forestry, claywork, pottery, carpentry, smithing, and road work. Everyone needed him. He became a consultant to the Liberian government and other leaders. With all these skills, he still felt the need to help in the spiritual realm!

With God's guidance, I handle medical and spiritual crises

Dr. Harley was gone much of the time, engaging in his consultant tasks, and Mildred was now very busy with a literacy program for those who spoke the Mano language. She had been teaching English to the school children. Influenced by the internationally-known missionary and literary expert, Dr. Frank Laubach, she started working with Liberian women in the villages. Dr. Laubach, who visited Liberia in the late forties and early fifties, saw the great need for people to be able to read and pioneered a system of phonetic teaching in native languages. His motto was "Each One Teach One." When Mildred taught one local woman to read, that woman in turn would teach another. It was a very successful program.

I was now left with our Liberian staff to make decisions. As time went on I was able to get a few of the local people together and start a class on patient care and nursing skills. At the same time I had to learn their ways and customs. For example, in the hospital, relatives came to stay with the patients and cook for them, frequently sleeping under their beds at night. Before long I fell in love with the Liberian people as all the missionaries seemed to do.

Each day was a routine of patient care. Dr. Harley's reputation had spread over the years; he was known far and wide. People walked for days to get to his clinic. Patients came in on crutches, were carried in hammocks, or even crawled to get there. One day when I was alone with only a 14-year-old boy to help me, a woman in labor was brought in. We helped her onto the table and discovered that one of the baby's legs had arrived. I had never handled such a challenge alone. I could only pray and ask God to give me wisdom and guidance to care for her. At that very moment a car with four doctors arrived on the mission compound from Monrovia. I sent the boy out to ask one of the doctors to come and help us. Dr. Poindexter, who was acquainted with Dr. Harley, came in. I thought he would scrub, but no such luck. He told me to proceed while he watched. I was able to deliver the baby in fine shape. A while later I was told that the woman who had given birth had intentionally broken her water and initiated the birth. She was a woman of some importance in the area, and it would have been politically bad as well as sad if the child had died. Praise God, all went well!

In another instance Dr. Harley asked me to accompany him to the village to

Good Friday, 1951. Two men who burned their fetishes

116

assist with a complication following childbirth. I grabbed my sterile package and went with him. When we arrived at the hut, he told me that the woman had a retained placenta. Men were not allowed in a hut during childbirth, another local tradition I learned very quickly. Dr. Harley sent me inside, while he stood outside the door! I found the patient lying on the dirt floor on some rags drenched in blood. Fortunately with very little help the placenta was loosened and delivered, and the bleeding stopped.

One more incident involved a woman with a big slash on her neck and several smaller cuts on her left arm. She was brought in on a stretcher. Luckily our new little surgical area was open. The young men, whom Dr. Harley had trained, sewed the woman up, and we eased her into bed. We were told that the woman's husband had been gone for three years. He had returned to find her living with another man. In anger, he attacked his wife and then committed suicide. That was not the end of the story, however. At 10:00 o'clock that night I was called to the clinic. The woman's husband had been brought in. While he had slit his throat from ear to ear, he was still alive! We did our best to sew him up, but it did not look as if he would survive. We put him in a bed in the other available room. We were not well equipped to take care of two inpatients, so the woman's brother stayed day and night with his sister to help with her care.

At times like these we were given opportunities to witness and tell of Jesus. A friend from Milwaukee, Wisconsin, had given me a set of Bible picture books. I brought these over from my room and presented the gospel to the woman's brother. He spoke English and was very eager to hear the Bible stories. He became a Christian. Meanwhile, in the other room, we did what we could to care for the man who had slashed his neck. He needed someone to stay with him. After the woman recovered sufficiently to be alone, I asked the young man if he would go in to help his brother-in-law. He responded that according to their customs, he could not help the man who had tried to kill his sister. I then explained to him that a Christian could always help through God's love. I was amazed to see his willingness to try to follow the teachings of Jesus, and he went in to help his brother-in-law. The husband also spoke enough English to communicate with me. Like his brother-in-law, he wanted to become a Christian. I tried to explain to him that God would forgive his sins when he confessed them and repented, but that he would still have to face the consequences of his actions. He seemed to understand. We surrounded both of our patients with prayer, and wonder of wonders, they both were healed and returned home.

I went to the Leprosy Colony to help out when needed. The treatment center also was used as a chapel, and services were held there regularly. On the morning of Good Friday one year, I was asked to lead the service. I did this through the use of an interpreter. That afternoon as I was resting at home, two men appeared at my door and asked me to return to the colony. Two of the patients wanted to become Christians and wanted to burn their fetishes, which were inanimate objects believed by some to possess magical powers. I had not mentioned this topic in any way during the service, so I was rather surprised.

Staff at Ganta Mission in 1949

I sent for Britt, and the two of us returned together. The Reverend Britt led the ceremony while the two men built a fire and burned the fetishes which they previously thought would help them. They now understood that only God could do so.

My responsibilities change

After I had been in Liberia for nine months, Dr. Hyla Waters came to Ganta Mission. She was an experienced American surgeon, who had been the head of a hospital in Wuhu, China, where she had worked under more sophisticated circumstances. Hyla was very eager to begin work, and I was relieved of responsibilities that were more appropriate for a physician. I had to re-adjust to a completely different situation, and at times it was very difficult to know what to do and what not to do. I tried to concentrate on patient care and the needs of the staff, while Hyla became the head of the hospital staff. I continued to go on rounds, taught the young people, and worked on the never-ending sterilization procedures. I was also now free to accompany Britt on some of his mission trips to the village, which I thoroughly enjoyed. On these trips, we would try to become acquainted with the local people and create an atmosphere of friendliness. With all of us sitting on pieces of wood in a circle in front of the huts, Pastor Britt would hold informal religious services introducing the families to the gospel.

118

Sei Punagbea, the little boy on the other boy's back, is now a retired surgeon and is living in the United States

Dr. Waters was like Dr. Harley in her quest for knowledge and information about everything in Liberia. She was interested in astronomy, and I learned much from her. It was natural for Hyla, who was so eager to learn and understand the customs and traditions of the people, to seek advice from Mildred, who had spent many years working in Liberia. However, I felt more isolated.

119

Our living situation contributed to my feeling of isolation. Hyla moved into Haffen House with Mildred, and sleeping quarters were provided for me in the upper story of a building under construction. The building would become a residence for hospital staff. We did not have air conditioning, and the heat up in my attic was almost intolerable at times. I moved all of my belongings into the attic but continued to share meals with Mildred and Hyla in Haffen House where we took turns supervising the cook.

Dining with a monkey!

There were always guests traveling through the country and staying at the mission with different families. Mostly they stayed at the Stone House with the Harleys who had made many friends from all over the world. Martha and B. B. Cofield never seemed to get tired of being good to people, and they had many guests also. The Haffen House was too small to have overnight guests, but we did offer some of them meals. One day a Danish couple, who were involved in a research project, stopped to have lunch with Mildred and me. They brought along their pet monkey, who also occupied a place at our table. All went peacefully. That was the first and only meal I ever shared with a monkey!

"What will happen to our children when you go?"

After I had been at Ganta Mission for two years, unrest was brewing in the Middle East, and I began to realize that I needed to re-establish my American citizenship. I was traveling on a Danish passport. One of the many visitors who passed through Ganta advised me to go to Monrovia to sign my name on the long quota list of people who were seeking American citizenship. I drove down to the city in the next truck headed in that direction, signed my name on the list, and returned to finish my term at Ganta.

I was beginning to feel drained physically and spiritually and finally came to the conclusion that I should not agree to a second term before I had an opportunity for further education and rest. I knew by then what I wanted to do in the future - to focus my efforts on training nurses.

As I packed to leave and then went to the clinic to say goodbye, it was a heart-breaking, yet encouraging, experience to see mothers sitting on the porch waiting for me. They had walked a long way to get there. One of them tearfully said, "What will happen to our children when you go?" Children had always been cared for at the mission, but we were all needed to reach out to more of them and to allocate additional time to address their needs. I comforted the mothers with the knowledge that two American nurses, who had been working in China, had arrived to take over the work.

120

11

New directions

And everyone who has left houses or brothers or sisters or father or mother or children or fields for my sake will receive a hundred times as much and will inherit eternal life. Matthew 19:29 (NIV).

The door opens for further education

On my way back to Denmark while waiting in the port city of Monrovia and visiting friends from other missions, I met a Danish scientist. He said that he had visited Ganta Mission and was very impressed with our work. He asked me if I was coming back. I told him that I hoped to rest for a while and obtain a little more education. Of course, I did not yet know how further education would come about. He took a notebook out of his pocket, tore off a sheet, wrote a few lines on it, and gave it to me. He told me to take the note to a professor whom he identified at the University of Aarhus. That slip of paper was instrumental in giving me access to the university for a course in nursing instruction and opened the door for my sister Marie to go also. She took a course in administration.

It was wonderful to be home with the family again. Shortly after I returned, my father showed me an article in a newspaper which was a slap in the face to those who had left their homes to toil in the missions. It accused missionaries of exploiting indigenous people, who just became "rice Christians," i.e., not true believers, but people who followed Christian leaders in order to obtain material goods. My father wrote a reply on what the missionaries really brought to people. No more articles on the subject appeared in our paper.

September 1, 1952, found Marie and me bicycling across the city to start our new educational adventure. The courses in which we were enrolled had quite recently been added to the curriculum to assist R.N.s who had been working in the field as we had. We gained many new friends. One drawback that we both had to overcome was the tight quarters we had to share for sleep and work. We both stayed with our parents who had very little extra room except for "heart room," as our mother called it.

Marie becomes supervisor of Bethesda

We both graduated in June, 1953. Neither Marie nor I were sure how we would use our newly acquired knowledge. Soon Marie was asked to be the supervisor of Bethesda, a home in Aarhus for unwed mothers and children from birth to age four. She hesitated in accepting the position. For some reason she always felt incompetent. Finally she gave in. During the summer of 1953 she assumed responsibility for the home, stipulating that she would do so only if she could change things as she saw fit. In a few years everything was changed! Financial development resulted with funds being supplied for complete remodeling of the interior of the home. The children were divided into small "families" consisting of four children of different ages. Consistency in staffing was established so nurses cared for the same children each day and acted as their "mothers." The children were dressed in cheerful clothing, all fitting the individual child. The remodeling was finished in 1956. One month later Queen Ingrid visited the home. Marie retired in 1973 after 20 years of service. At the recommendation of the board, the Queen honored her with a medal for good work.

Marie used money that she was given at her retirement to visit her "daughter," Araksie, and her family who lived in Brazil. She had money left from her mission work in Greece which she used to help the family buy a small business in Argentina. Later the family moved to San Francisco.

I resign from the mission

I was asked to teach preschool nursing for about 15 young girls who had applied for acceptance into St. Luke's School of Nursing in Copenhagen. The course lasted three months before the students took their entrance exams. All the girls passed, and as I write this in 1998, some are still employed there. The time I spent at St. Luke's Institute was very enjoyable, but my contract was for only three months. I did not have any idea what my next move would be, but I kept feeling the urge to resign from my mission board. Finally one day I went to the board and told them that I wanted to sever my relationship with them and be on my own. Although it seemed like the right decision, I went home and wept for a long time.

A job offer in Liberia

The next day, I received a letter from the Liberian Mining Company, an American business, asking me to accept a nursing position with them. Some

122

of my friends at Ganta Mission had suggested me as a candidate. I really did not think I could or should accept this position. Then a few days later, I received a telephone call. An American man invited me to dinner along with two of his male companions in a hotel in Copenhagen. I told him I would think about his invitation and call him back. I was feeling a little uneasy about this dinner since I did not know any of the men. I finally decided to accept if I could bring along my friend from the diocese, Sister Karen. Karen did not speak English but could be with me as a support. Two of the gentlemen were lawyers, and one was a banker. They had been in Liberia to examine possibilities for business investments after the war. The U.S. had developed a port in Liberia during World War II; now American businessmen were discovering the assets of the country. The men had been in contact with the Liberian Mining Company and had carried a letter from the company to me. They encouraged me to accept the job.

The successful mining company, which was a division of Republic Steel, mined some of the very finest iron ore. It was located in Bomi Hills where a good-sized community of people from Europe and the U.S lived. A railroad had been built from Monrovia to Bomi Hills in order to transfer the ore, and a new hospital had just been completed. The hospital needed to be equipped, from the very building itself to the staff, and procedures developed to ensure a well-run facility. There were two doctors, but a nurse, who was acquainted with the local people and capable of leading the nursing staff, was needed to head up the project. The mining company was eager to open the hospital.

U.S. Citizenship

Immediately in the wake of receiving the job offer in Liberia, notice came from the American Embassy that I was next in line to get my American citizenship established. Having been born in the U.S., I actually was an American citizen, but this fact was not clear at the time. I had no papers to prove my U.S. citizenship, and in the post-war confusion I was considered Danish, since I traveled under a Danish passport. Now I wondered how everything was going to fall into place. If I did not take my turn in the quota list, I would lose my place. I thought back on that day two years before, when I felt I should apply for U.S. citizenship. Also, it was November, and I wanted so much to spend Christmas with my family. I really had no choice, however, if I wanted U.S. citizenship. I wrote a letter to the Liberian Mining Company explaining the situation and prepared to leave for America. I shared my regrets with my family over the lost holiday with them but promised that I would return for my parents' fiftieth wedding anniversary.

I returned to Cambridge, Wisconsin, and as I had done several times before, stayed with my friend Ardelle and her mother, "Grandma Jarlsberg." They were so good to me. I am sure it was not always easy to have an extra person in their home. The citizenship application stipulated that there is a five-year waiting period following registration. I worked for a month in a nursing home

At Bomi Hills, Liberia Mining Company, Dagmar with two nurses

At Bomi Hills, Liberia Mining Company Hospital, Dagmar
with Dr. Sekenene and Dr. Ross

124

in the nearby city of Madison but did not feel at all that this was the job for me. It seemed as if the door to my future was closed, and I had no light on the subject whatsoever. A telegram came from the mining company; again I replied by explaining my situation. I waited for direction. Neither option seemed right - going to Bomi Hills or remaining in Cambridge to establish my citizenship. I continued to wait. I made my decision after receiving a third letter from the mining company. The company had been in touch with the immigration office and told me that I would not lose my place on the list if I came to work for them and that time in Liberia would count as part of the five-year waiting period. I was headed back to Liberia!

A fine Christian man

In the meantime, I had become acquainted with a lovely family - Joe Vasby and his five children, Marilyn, Joyce, Owen, Lucille, and Philip, who were between the ages of seventeen and seven. Joe's wife, Clarice, had died a year before. She was Grandma Jarlsberg's daughter, Ardelle's sister. On Sundays Joe and his children often came to dinner and would spend the afternoon with us. One day Grandma Jarlsberg said, "Now there's a good man for you - if he didn't have so many kids." "Wow," I thought, although I did not answer her, "little does she know that if I did marry, it would be for the sake of the children." I had seen enough of this family to know that they were easy to love. I felt so sorry for them, having lost their mother. More and more I admired Joe, and he was extremely courteous to me. I knew he was a fine Christian man. When I had first met him, I had been touched by a heartfelt prayer that he had offered in church. Our friendship deepened without our sharing any words about it.

Then one day Joe asked me for a date. We took a ride around the countryside and returned to his kitchen where he served his favorite ice cream. Earlier, he had spent eight years with Golden Guernsey Dairy in Milwaukee making ice cream.

Joe and I began to consider the possibility of marriage. Unknown to each other, we both had similar dreams during this time. My dream was as real to me as the one I had experienced years earlier about Lake Baikal in Russia before I went to China. The dream left me with the feeling that we belonged together. Of course, we both prayed about God's will for some time. I had, however, already accepted the job with the Liberian Mining Company, and I was scheduled to leave shortly.

I return to nursing in Liberia

On a cold winter day, February 3, 1954, Joe and two of his children drove me to the airport. I felt a repeat of all the painful goodbyes I had experienced over the years. Once again, I was entering into a completely different place where everyone was new to me. I was not headed to a Danish hospital or a well-known mission hospital, but an up-to-date American one. Could I handle the situation? I reasoned that I would be serving under the same Father in Heaven, so I dared give it a try.

I arrived during the dry season in Liberia. I was dressed in a warm suit and felt ready to melt when I landed. A couple of men from the mining company were there to meet me. There was not much conversation on the way to Bomi Hills, but one of them gave me a good idea of what was expected of me. He rather suddenly and surprisingly said, "Remember, this is not a mission station," implying that they needed a nurse but not a missionary. I believe God gave me the answer as I replied, "Remember, I did not ask to come." No more was said on the subject.

My time in Bomi Hills was interesting, but demanding. I lived in the hospital and worked day and night. If ever I felt that I was a "Jack of all trades and master of none," it was here. I was involved with all tasks, from sewing curtains to setting up the nurses' schedules. The hospital had been built for the large mining community, so most of the patients were white employees of the mining company; however, there was also a ward for local black patients. There were no patients when I arrived, but that did not last long. Soon emergency situations landed on our doorstep. While in the midsts of hiring local staff and establishing schedules, we performed surgical procedures and delivered babies . Equipment arrived piecemeal. Gradually everything came together.

Despite the admonition when I arrived that I was not hired as a missionary, the hospital made good use of my skills in this area as well. I held devotions for the staff in the morning and talked and prayed with the patients throughout the day. One Sunday I left the hospital a little late for worship service in the chapel. The minister did not arrive, and they asked me, still wearing my nursing uniform, to lead the service! In short, Bomi Hills made good use of all 26 years of my previous experience.

I decide to marry Joe

The people of the Bomi Hills community were very kind to me, and the general manager, Charles Dewey, and his wife were very considerate. We soon became good friends. It was during these months that I had to make up my mind about marrying Joe. I wrote a letter to each of the children asking them if they wanted me for a mother. Four of them answered promptly, but the fifth wanted time to think things through, as he always does. Finally his response came also. I did not tell the mining company of my plans, because I still felt a little uncertain. How would I fit into a farmer's life when I had never lived on a farm? I was brought up in a parsonage and worked in the medical community all my life. Again I faced the unknown. It was only as the mining company began to pressure me to sign a two-year contract that I had to tell them I had decided to get married. Mr. Dewey, who worked hard to encourage me to sign the contract, was a real gentleman. When he realized my position, he did all he could to help me.

I asked that I be relieved of my duties in time to travel to Denmark for the celebration of my parents' fiftieth wedding anniversary. The good salary that I received during my five months' stay at Bomi Hills made it possible for me to completely renew my wardrobe. I needed this desperately, since I had lived in uniforms for years. Not only did the staff wish me well, but they planned a going away party and a shower for me! I felt overwhelmed by their friendship and almost regretted my decision to leave. I later bought Danish china for my new home with money I received from the party.

I left for Monrovia on June 28, 1954. While waiting for my passage to Denmark, I met several good friends and said more good-byes. While I was in Monrovia, the American Ambassador to Liberia and his wife very unexpectedly gave a dinner for 26 guests in my honor!

Stranded in Dakar

Thinking that I had my transportation all in order, I was very surprised to be put off the plane in Dakar, Senegal, at 8:00 P.M. I was told that there was some mistake, that I was not booked to go further on that plane. At first there was no one who could speak English, so I just sat on a bench out in the open on that tropical evening. I felt perfectly at peace and just waited. This episode seemed similar to one my mother had experienced when she became lost in Boston in 1903. She had come to the U.S. from Denmark to marry my father and was staying with friends. One day she ventured out on her own while doing some errand, and she lost her way back. She could not speak any English, and no one could understand Danish. She decided that she would just sit in the train station until Dad found her. In the meantime, Dad was looking all over for her. He called the station and asked if they had seen a young Danish woman. "No," they answered, "there is only an Italian deaf, mute woman sitting here." The deaf, mute Italian woman was actually my black-haired Danish mother, who could not speak English! Lucky for Mother, Dad came to the station to see for himself!

While I sat on my bench in the warm summer night, a Norwegian captain, who had been contacted, came to talk with me. That little interlude gave me a first class ticket to Copenhagen with a 24 hour layover in Zurich, Switzerland. I enjoyed beautiful hotel accommodations, a tour of Zurich, and a chance to do a little shopping. The trip over Germany was beautiful. I arrived in Kastrup Airport, Copenhagen, at 7:00 P.M. on July 5, 1954. I called Dad and Mother from the train station and then took the train to Hellerup to visit Sister Karen and other friends. I caught a sleeper train home that night. There I was greeted by Mother and Dad, my sister, Helga, and her husband Ernst, and their three sons, Torben, Finn, and Mogens. This concluded another section of my life, and a whole new one was about to begin!

50th wedding anniversary of Laura and Niels Christian Petersen, 1954

Where can we marry?

Joe had written to me in Liberia and asked me where I wanted to be married. I answered, "The only guidance I have is that we meet in Denmark and ask Dad to marry us." He replied, "I am sorry I cannot please you in that; I have my back against a wall at this time." I prayed about other possibilities and wrote to my friend, B. B. Cofield for advice. Then Dr. Hyla Waters suggested that her brother, who was a pastor in New York, marry us. As it turned out, the New York pastor was on a trip at the time and unavailable. Also, Joe's family encouraged him to come to Denmark to be married by my father. I had wished to have Joe come to the big day in our family - the golden wedding anniversary on July 12. I thought that Joe and I could have a quiet ceremony late in the afternoon of that day. This plan, however, did not meet with the approval of my family. July 12 was Dad and Mother's special day! As the event played out, it had been impossible for Joe to arrange to come on that day.

Laura and Christian's fiftieth anniversary

The fiftieth anniversary was an unforgettable family day. The Danes know how to celebrate! A hall was rented for the dinner. Beautiful decorations with candles and flowers festooned the tables. Telegrams, greetings, and beautiful bouquets of flowers came in throughout the day, along with family and friends. On such occasions, songs are written in honor of the couple. The meals at such events sometimes last for four hours. Many speeches are made in tribute to the couple. When my father finally rose to respond, he began with a hearty thank

128

you to all who had made their day so special and also to those who had stood by them throughout the years. Of course, one thing that I could not forget was his joy over the fact that all seven of their children who were living, along with their families, were in attendance. He remembered those family members who had been taken from them earlier through death. Then he said, "And when Dagmar some time ago promised she would be here for our day, I had my doubts. I could not see how it would be, but she is here!" How thankful I was that I had come and also glad that it was their special day only, without my wedding adding distraction.

Joe and I marry

Another wedding date was set and planned when Joe wrote that his flight had been cancelled. We tried again. This time we planned for Monday, August 23, in the Cathedral of Aarhus where my father received the honor of assisting for nine months as an interim pastor. In the meantime I had been very busy taking care of my wardrobe, seeing friends, and getting ready for my big move to the States. I felt great in my new suit and my matching hat and accessories when I went to Copenhagen to meet Joe at the airport on August 21. He did not arrive on the expected plane, so I waited until the last one from the U.S. taxied in. I watched as the arrivals walked off the plane. I did not see Joe. When the last person had deplaned, I turned away to decide what I should do next. Then he came up behind me and said teasingly, "You were really looking for me, weren't you?" To this day I have no idea how he managed to elude me. I am sure he planned it that way. We stayed in one of the hotels and caught a flight the next day to Aarhus.

On August 23 we were married in the Cathedral in Aarhus. What a privilege to have my 78-year-old father perform the ceremony! The family had arranged a beautiful occasion for us. There was a formal dinner with the tables decorated with many flowers. There were songs and speeches as on Dad and Mother's special day. I was disappointed that Joe could not stay more than a day, as our honeymoon was planned as a trip to Norway. Joe had never visited his relatives in Stavanger. We had two very good days sailing up the fjords and visiting his aunts, uncles, and cousins. Then the trip turned westward. Once again I came to Cambridge, Wisconsin. This time to stay.

Wedding picture, Dagmar and Joe Vasby, August 23, 1954

Epilogue
Special Friends

The impact of friends

In the process of writing this story, I have renewed my acquaintance with friends around the world, and it has thrilled my heart. Going through pictures that have been stored away in boxes has greatly enlivened the realization of the impact of these friends upon my life. I am thankful for each one of them. At times I feel like I want to keep on writing just to experience them all again.

Before I close, I want to give you sketches of just a few of these special people and to share another example of my parents' continuing influence on my life.

Congregation members

As a P.K., I have a special appreciation for people in my father's congregations who accepted and remembered our family with thoughtfulness, especially in times of need. There were many such wonderful people. I would like to share anecdotes about two of them.

I was eleven years old when the Spanish Flu epidemic hit the country in 1918, taking so many lives. One of my teachers died after being ill only a few days. Very few people escaped illness. This was also the case in our family. At one point, only Dad was well enough to wait on the rest of us. Then he also got sick. One night stands out in my mind. Dad and Mother were anxiously caring for my little brother, who was fighting for his very life. At two o'clock in the morning, there was a knock on the bedroom window. Emma Christiansen, a middle-aged woman from our church, wanted to know if she could help us. She had felt a very urgent concern for us and had walked from town out to the parsonage in the dark night, risking her own life to help us. Needless to say, none of us ever forgot her.

A more humorous event took place when I was a bit younger. Our family was invited to dinner at the home of one of the families in the congregation. Topsy gladly trotted off pulling the wagon of happy children. Then some of us overheard Dad say to Mother, "Are you sure, Mother, that we were all invited, or was it just you and I?" Mother replied, "Why, yes, I am sure that was the idea." My parents became awfully quiet. Marie and I were very embarrassed to think that maybe we should not have been along. We were rather subdued for the rest of the ride. What a relief when we arrived and were all greeted with wide open arms. How we loved those people!

Dr. Li Wei Yen

Dr. Li Wei Yen was one of the truly unforgettable and remarkable people who came into my life. I had the privilege of working hand-in-hand with her during the last three years that I was in China. We worked together when the struggle for supremacy in China was at its peak, first between the Chinese and Japanese armies, later between the Chinese nationalists led by Chiang Kai-shek and Mao Tse-tung's 8th Army.

Dr. Li was a petite beautiful young woman, who studied medicine in Peking. While in that city, she had become a Christian, although none of her wealthy family were Christians. When the Japanese took Peking, she moved to Mukden in Manchuria to the Scotch Presbyterian Medical College. About the time that I moved from Hsin Ching to Antung, Dr. Li was hired by the Danish Mission Hospital to serve there together with Dr. Bi and her sister. These women were beautiful Christians, whose lives and testimonies were very influential during this time. Dr. Li and I met for prayer every morning before joining the other staff for devotions and then work. After a difficult day in surgery, Dr. Li would slip a hard-boiled egg into my pocket as a special treat.

After I left China, Dr. Li continued her work in Antung for a short period of time. When the Communists took over Antung, the hospital was ransacked and looted. It was an impossible struggle to keep the institution running. Staff fled. Dr. Li moved back north to Mukden but soon had to flee again. Dr. Li knew that her letters would be read and censored. Still during her correspondence over the next two years, she told of her desire to serve the Lord wherever she was sent. One of her brothers became a Christian during this time. Gradually all news from Dr. Li stopped. I knew this meant that she was no longer on this earth but had received her reward in heaven. I remember and honor Dr. Li for her concern for the sick, young and old alike, which absorbed her under any conditions she was placed.

Dr. Wilfred S. Boayue

Four shouts by a Liberian midwife announced the birth of a male child, Sei Punagbea Boayue. Sei began life sometime between the years 1937-1939. The exact date is unknown since such records were not kept. Sei's father was a village chief who later became a clan chief. He had many wives, and Sei does not know how many siblings he has. For many years Sei was plagued by tropical diseases. The devotion of his mother changed the course of his life. Sei's mother carried him on her back twenty-five miles to Ganta Mission in order that he might receive medical care. They made these journeys weekly or sometimes twice a week.

Sei's father was a friend of Dr. Harley. The chief brought the boy to see the school at Ganta Mission, but Sei did not enter the school until a few months after the death of his father. One of his elder brothers brought him to the Ganta Mission Boys' School. He was baptized in 1949. Sei could not take part in lively games or play ball with the other boys, but he enjoyed reading and participated in the classes which trained staff to assist in the clinic. He was the smartest of his class. In 1950, around the age of eleven or twelve, he wrote an explanation of why he wanted to be a medical professional:

I really have not entirely decided what I want to be. My first choice was to be a minister. I wanted to help my people get rid of their false Gods - Wood God, Rain God, Sun God, Moon God and others - and to help them to follow our Lord and Savior, Jesus Christ. But now I have decided what I want to be. I see around me my people suffer from all sorts of diseases, and I know how much I have suffered. Therefore I understand that I must become a Christian doctor. Then I can treat their illnesses and teach them about our Lord and Savior, Jesus Christ. I want to be what the Lord wants me to be.

While a senior in high school, he wrote:

I dream of the day when I shall be prepared enough to answer the cry of my people .... I have suffered from these diseases .... know and trust that God who can send foreigners from their countries to help you, will doubtless make a way for you to help yourself. As you pray for Liberia, know that we here, think of you as friends or "our father's children" for that is the meaning of my tribe's word for friends.

After studying at the Ganta Mission school, Sei attended a Methodist high school in Monrovia where his high grades paid for his education. He changed his name from Sei Punagbea to Wilfred. Next he traveled to West Virginia for college and medical school. On February 27, 1972, he married Stella Mae Narcisse, an American woman whom he met at Tulane University where he was studying public health and tropical medicine. They have three sons and one daughter, all of whom were educated in the U.S. Dr. Boayue served for many years as a physician with the World Health Organization. He became the first Liberian physician to serve on the staff of Ganta Mission. Dr. Boayue returned to the U.S. in September, 1998, after serving twenty-seven years in Liberia and Zambia. He is looking forward to a new life in the U.S.

Christian and Laura Petersen

No one has left a more indelible impression on me than my parents. In the second career of my life as a wife and mother, my parents were as influential as they had been in my mission work. During the first years of my marriage, when I felt that I had no one to whom I could speak as puzzling situations arose, I would gaze out my kitchen window in the direction of Denmark and ask myself, "What would Dad and Mother do? How would they react?" I always came away with helpful insights!

My father had two mottos in life - to tell the truth in love, and when all is said and done, to God alone be the Glory. These mottos have remained with me throughout my life.

Even in death my parents were role models. My father passed away on September 14, 1959. For three years he had suffered from emphysema caused by heart failure. Mother was continually by his side during his suffering. Shortly before his death she heard him say, "I am getting a place all of my own." After his retirement his desk was in the corner of the small dining room in their retirement home. In this rather small house were many guests and some of us adult children who were always returning home. Perhaps we never really appreciated how much he had missed his private study. When near death, he experienced a bright light surrounding him. "How wonderful the light is!" he exclaimed. After Dad's death, Mother was asked, "How do you feel?" She replied, "I am so happy. All of my prayers were answered!" She had prayed for three things - that the Lord would give her strength to be there for her husband; that his mind would be kept clear and sane until his death; and that there would be light during his passing. Mother died three and a half years later on March 4, 1963.

In closing

Through nine decades I have enjoyed the interactions and memories of a host of family and friends around the world. Unmindful of nationality or skin color, such friendships grow stronger as time goes on. There is nothing comparable to the fellowship of true believers.

In closing, I would encourage all parents to create good memories for their children. With God all things are possible.

The last move

As I was leaving Ganta Mission, The Littlest Angels Sunday School Class presented me with the words to a song, entitled "The Last Move." I would like to leave you with the words to this song.

The Last Move

I've been traveling for Jesus so much of my life
I've been traveling on land and on sea
But I'm counting on taking a trip to the skies
That will be the last move for me.

When I move to the skies, up to heaven on high
What a wonderful trip that will be!
I'm all ready to go, washed in Calvary's flood
That will be the last move for me.

There'll be prophets of yore whom I'll meet over there
And whose teachings have guided me right
I shall meet the Apostles and Jesus my Lord
I believe I shall know at sight.

Here I'm bothered with packing each time that I move
And I carry a load in each hand
But I'll not need one thing I have used in this world
When I move to that heavenly land.
(author unknown)

Vasby family, 1955
Left to right: Marilyn, Philip, Dagmar, Lucille, Joe, Joyce and Owen

Joe and Dagmar Vasby with their children, 1980
Left to right: Joyce, Philip, Marilyn, Joe, Dagmar, Owen and Lucille

Grandchildren and great-grandchildren, May 19, 1993.
Family together after the funeral of Joe Vasby

Acknowledgements

A number of wonderful people have provided encouragement, support, and assistance during the process of creating this book. We gratefully acknowledge the contribution each of them has made toward the finished product. We thank God for their help.

All of the family and friends who, over the years, encouraged Dagmar to write her memoirs, including the women of the 7:00 A.M. exercise group in Cambridge, Wisconsin.

Randall Luchterhand for his support and encouragement, his cheerful and tireless offers to print manuscript drafts, and his computer consultation.

Hans Christian Gejlsbjerg and The Danish Missionary Society for permission to use "One Month in a Chinese Prison," written by Jacob Gejlsbjerg for inclusion in the book, *Sunrays from a Time of Darkness*, published in 1946.

Wilfred Boayue for permission to share anecdotes from his life story.

Howard Hovde for his heart-felt forward to the book and his review of the manuscript draft.

Myrvin F. Christopherson for his thoughtful forward to the book.

The following for their encouragement and careful review of the manuscript draft:

Mark Behrendt
Jim Biechler
Nancy Brackebusch
Helga Frandsen
Greg Gullicksrud
Gene Moen
Alma Petersen
Richard Petersen
Rose Marie Ward

Linda and Mark Wilfer for their translations of documents from Chinese to English.

Carl and Eleanora Moen for their interest and encouragement during the writing process.

The following for their assistance and consultation during the process of locating a publisher:

Marshall Cook
Don Jorgensen
Michael Messina
Tom Moe

Tony Schweitzer for the use of his computer during our search for a publisher.

Gratefully,
Dagmar and Charlene

138

Glossary

Axminster rug - a high quality English carpet machine-woven with pile tufts inserted mechanically in a variety of textures and patterns

Bible women - Chinese Christian women who minister to the people and help spread the gospel

blomster - Danish word for flowers

bøger - Danish word for books

børn - Danish word for children

Chinese communists - also known as the 8th Army; leader - Mao Zedong; fought civil war with Chinese nationalists

Chinese nationalists - also known as the Kuomintang; leader - Chiang Kai-shek; fought civil war with Chinese communists

constitutional monarchy - government ruled by a king or queen whose power is limited by a constitution. In Denmark, the king is the executive power, the king in conjunction with the Rigsdag (parliament) is the legislative branch, and the judicial power rests with the Courts of Justice.

gaardsplads - courtyard of a Danish farm, surrounded by the home and farm buildings

Gestapo - secret police who often use underhanded and terrorist methods against people who they accuse of treason or rebellion against authority

Jutland - peninsula north of Germany that forms the continental portion of Denmark

kang - type of bed used in northern China; warmed by heat from a cooking kettle in the kitchen directed into flues under the bed

kao-liang **porridge** - a cereal made of sorghum grain; it is common in China and eaten when rice is scarce

krone - (Kroner - plural) - Danish dollar

Lake Baikal - lake in Russia that is the largest freshwater lake in Eurasia and the deepest lake in the world *li* - Chinese measure of distance equal to about one third of a mile

living lights - (Danish) burning candles on a Christmas tree

mien chiaotze - a noodle-like Chinese delicacy made of wheat flour

no-man's-land - area between territory occupied by the Chinese communists and land held by the Chinese nationalists

P.K.s - preacher's kids

pogroms - organized persecution and massacres

rice Christians - not true believers, but people who follow Christian leaders in order to   obtain material goods

rickshaw - a small two-wheeled vehicle usually for one passenger pulled by one man; used first in Japan

Shinto - Japanese sun goddess; religion of Japan consisting of cult-like devotion to deities of natural forces and honoring the Emperor as a descendant of the sun goddess

Trans-Siberian Railroad - rail line extending from Europe to the Pacific Ocean

UNRRA - United Nations Relief and Rehabilitation Administration; agency founded in 1943to give aid to countries liberated from Germany, Japan, Italy and other Axis countries

yamen - the police headquarters in China

yen - Japanese or Chinese dollar

References

Gejlsbjerg, J. (1946). "One Month in a Chinese Prison." *In Sunrays from a Time of Darkness.* Hellerup, Denmark: The Danish Missionary Society.

Other books by Lur Publications

Tante Johanne
Letters of a Danish Immigrant Family
1887-1910
Letters and photographs with commentary by John W. Nielsen
118 pp. ISBN 0-930697-01-4
$12.95 plus shipping

Many Danes, Some Norwegians
Karen Miller's Diary - 1894
With photographs and commentary by John W. Nielsen
173 pp. ISBN 0-930697-02-2
$14.95 plus shipping

A Frame but No Picture
The story of a boy left behind in Denmark
Edited by John W. Nielsen
63 pp. ISBN 0-930697-03-0
$8.50 plus shipping

Embracing Two Worlds:
The Thorvald Muller Family of Kimballton
Edited by Barbara Lund-Jones & John W. Nielsen
180 pp. ISBN 0-930697-04-9
$14.95 plus shipping

Passages from India:
Letters, Essays, and Poems
1944-1946
by Norman C. Bansen
201 pp. ISBN 0-930697-05-7
$19.95 plus shipping

Boats in the Night
Knud Dyby's Story of Resistance and Rescue
by Martha Loeffler
140 pp. ISBN 0-930697-07-3
$14.95 plus shipping

Our Last Frontiers:
A World Cruise Diary
by Borge and Lotte Christensen
238 pp. ISBN 0-930697-08-1
$22.50 plus shipping

Order from: Lur Publications
Danish Immigrant Archive
Dana College
Blair, Nebraska 68008

Lur Publications takes its name from the graceful bronze age horns found in Scandinavian museums. Just as today when those horns are blown, sounds from an ancient past are heard, so these books give voice to a less distant Danish past.

Lur Publications Policies

Lur Publications is committed to the publication of materials that relate to the Danish American experience. To achieve this goal it encourages research and scholarship on Danish immigrant subjects, on the life and contributions of their descendants, and on connections between Denmark and Danes abroad. Significant in achieving this goal is making available to the general public materials in the Danish Immigrant Archive - Dana College. In its basic purpose Lur Publications complements the goals of the Danish American Heritage Society.

A further aim is to promote the collection, preservation, cataloging and use of written materials produced and received by Danish immigrants and their descendants. Such materials are welcomed by the respective Danish Immigrant Archives located at Dana College and Grand View College. Artifacts associated with Danish immigrants are sought by the Danish Immigrant Museum in Elk Horn, Iowa.

Scholars wishing to submit manuscripts for consideration are invited to contact Lur Publications, Danish Immigrant Archive, Dana College, Blair, Nebraska 68008-1041, (402) 426-7910, FAX: (402) 426-7332, e-mail: jwnielse@acad2.dana.edu

 Lur Publications Personnel

General Editor: Dr. John W. Nielsen
Advisory Board: Dr. Myrvin Christopherson, James E. Corbly, Dr. Paul Formo, Dr. John Mark Nielsen, Ruth Rasmussen